MW01037562

To:

From:

365 Devotions to Inspire Your Day

hugs

Daily
Inspirations for
Grandmas

HOWARD BOOKS
A DIVISION OF SIMON & SCHUSTER
New York   London   Toronto   Sydney

Our purpose at Howard Books is to:
- *Increase faith* in the hearts of growing Christians
- *Inspire holiness* in the lives of believers
- *Instill hope* in the hearts of struggling people everywhere
Because He's coming again!

Published by Howard Books, a division of Simon & Schuster, Inc.
1230 Avenue of the Americas, New York, NY 10020
www.howardpublishing.com

ISBN-13: 978-1-4391-1237-3
10 9 8 7 6 5 4 3 2 1

HOWARD and colophon are registered trademarks of Simon & Schuster, Inc.

Manufactured in China
For information regarding special discounts for bulk purchases, please
contact: Simon & Schuster Special Sales at 1-866-506-1949 or
business@simonandschuster.com.

The Simon & Schuster Speakers Bureau can bring authors to your live
event. For more information or to book an event, contact the Simon &
Schuster Speakers Bureau at 1-866-248-3049 or visit our website at
www.simonspeakers.com.

Compiled by Criswell Freeman
Cover design by Tennille Paden
Interior design by Bart Dawson
Photography—January Photo: © Gornist | Dreamstime.com; February
Photo: © Mrgreen | Dreamstime.com; March Photo: M and M Inc | Digital
Vision; April Photo: © Sandralise | Dreamstime.com; May Photo: © Galdzer
| Dreamstime.com; June Photo: © Imigra | Dreamstime.com; July Photo: ©
Gvictoria | Dreamstime.com; August Photo: © Hagenla | Dreamstime.com;
September Photo: © Sandralise | Dreamstime.com; October Photo: © Britvich
| Dreamstime.com; November Photo: © Georgeburba | Dreamstime.com;
December Photo: © Hartemink | Dreamstime.com

Let nothing disturb you,
nothing frighten you;
all things are passing;
God never changes.

—St. Teresa of Ávila

Introduction

Back in the good old days, it was easy to stereotype grandmothers because most grandmoms had both feet planted firmly in the past. But no more. Today, grandmothers are staying younger longer by staying connected, staying involved, staying informed, and keeping both feet planted squarely in the present. This book celebrates the gifts and the contributions of today's thoroughly modern grandmothers, whether they're 41 or 101.

As a grandparent, you are keenly aware that God has blessed you with a profound gift: your family. And as a citizen of the twenty-first century, you're also aware of the many opportunities that confront you, opportunities that would have been largely unknown to women of previous generations. These pages are intended to serve as an inspirational reminder of these opportunities and of the fun times that lie before you as you give—and receive—as many hugs as possible throughout each day.

The fabric of daily life is woven with the threads of habit, and no habit is more important than the habit of consistent prayer and daily devotion to God. This text provides 365 chances for you to celebrate God's gifts and to give thanks for blessings. When you do, you will worship your Creator, not just with words, but also with deeds. And then, just as He has promised, God will most certainly smile upon you and yours . . . now and forever.

January

Thank-You Hug for Grandmother

Dear Grandmother,

As the new year begins, we pause to think about the years that have passed—and all the things you've done for our family and for our world. You've worked so hard and made so many sacrifices that we cannot begin to thank you for each and every act of kindness. You've simply given us more gifts than we could ever count. But even if we can't count your gifts, we know why you gave them—love. And please don't ever forget that we love you too . . . now and forever.

A Grandmother Is . . .

Her children rise up and call her blessed.
Proverbs 31:28 NKJV

A grandmother is many things: She is the matriarch of the family, its keeper of traditions, its historian, and its mentor. A grandmother is a spiritual guide, a role model, a trusted friend, and a beloved family treasure. A grandmother cares for her loved ones and lights the way for future generations by sharing her wisdom, her concerns, her hopes, her faith, and, above all, her love.

A grandmother's love extends beyond time and space, weaving itself as an unbroken thread through future generations. In truth, a grandmother's influence upon her family lasts a lifetime . . . and beyond.

On the pages that follow, we shall consider the important role of that singular woman without whom the family would not—indeed could not—exist. That woman, of course, is Grandmother.

*I thank God for my grandmother who stood on
the word of God and lived with the spirit
of courage and grace.*
Maya Angelou

Embracing God's Love

*We know how much God loves us, and we have put
our trust in him. God is love, and all who live in love
live in God, and God lives in them.*

1 John 4:16 NLT

As a grandparent, you know the profound love
that you hold in your heart for your own family.
As a child of God, you can only imagine the infinite
love that your heavenly Father holds for you.

God made you in His own image, and now,
precisely because you are a wondrous creation
treasured by God, a question presents itself: What
will you do in response to the Creator's love? Will you
ignore it or embrace it? Will you return it or neglect
it? That decision, of course, is yours and yours alone.
But make no mistake: when you embrace God's
love, you are forever changed. You feel differently
about yourself, your neighbors, your family, and your
world.

Your heavenly Father—a God of infinite love and
mercy—is waiting to embrace you with open arms.
Accept His love today and forever.

God loves each of us as if there were only one of us.

St. Augustine

He Wants You to Serve

The greatest among you must be a servant.
But those who exalt themselves will be humbled,
and those who humble themselves will be exalted.
Matthew 23:11–12 NLT

As you seek to discover God's unfolding purpose for your life, you'll find yourself asking this question: How does God want me to serve my family and my community today?

Whatever your path, whatever your career, whatever your calling, you may be certain of this: service to others is an integral part of God's plan for your life.

Every single day of your life, including this one, God will give you opportunities to serve Him by serving His children and yours. Welcome those opportunities with open arms. They are God's gift to you, His way of allowing you to achieve greatness.

God wants you to serve with willing hands and a loving heart. And He will surely reward you for your willingness to share your talents and your time with your family and the world.

Some people give time, some give money, some their skills
and connections, some literally give their
life's blood. But everyone has something to give.
Barbara Bush

Thanking God for Your Blessings

I will make them and the area around My hill a blessing:
I will send down showers in their season—
showers of blessing.
Ezekiel 34:26 HCSB

Because you are a grandmother, you have been specially blessed by the Creator. And make no mistake: God has given you a happy assortment of treasures that are, in truth, simply too numerous to count. Your blessings include life, family, freedom, friends, talents, and possessions, for starters. But the list certainly doesn't stop there. And since you've received so much, the appropriate moment to thank the Creator for His generosity is always the present moment.

Of course, the gifts you receive from God are multiplied when you share them with others. So today, give thanks to God for your blessings, and demonstrate your gratitude by sharing those blessings with your loved ones, your friends, and the world. When you do, everybody wins.

Think of the blessings we so easily take for granted: Life
itself; preservation from danger; every bit of health we
enjoy; every hour of liberty; the ability
to see, to hear, to speak, to think, and to imagine
all this comes from the hand of God.
Billy Graham

Guard Your Thoughts

May the words of my mouth and the thoughts of my heart be pleasing to you, O LORD, my rock and my redeemer.

Psalm 19:14 NLT

Wise grandmothers understand that their thoughts have a tendency to transform themselves into reality. That's why a positive attitude pays such powerful dividends. Yet on occasion, all of us allow the worries of everyday life to overwhelm our thoughts and cloud our vision.

When we focus on the frustrations of today or the uncertainties of tomorrow, we rob ourselves of peace in the present moment. But, when we focus on God's grace, and when we trust in the ultimate wisdom of God's plan for our lives, our worries no longer tyrannize us.

Today, Grandmother, remember that God is infinitely greater than the challenges you face. And remember that your thoughts are profoundly powerful; so guard them accordingly.

Believe that your tender, loving thoughts and wishes for good have the power to help the struggling souls of the earth rise higher.

Ella Wheeler Wilcox

Praying for Plenty of Patience

Always be humble, gentle, and patient,
accepting each other in love.
Ephesians 4:2 NVC

The rigors of family life can test the patience of the most even-tempered grandmothers, because, from time to time, even the most mannerly children and grandchildren may do things that are worrisome or troublesome or both. Why? Because children and grandchildren, like the more senior members of their clans, are decidedly imperfect.

So what's a grandmother to do? Well, for starters, savvy grandmoms pray for patience, plenty of patience. And if emotion-purging anger is about to erupt, wise grandmothers hold their tongues and count to a thousand, if necessary.

Sometimes, patience is the price we pay for being responsible, mature adults, and that's as it should be. After all, think how patient our heavenly Father has been with us.

When my kids become wild and unruly,
I use a nice, safe playpen.
When they're finished, I climb out.
Erma Bombeck

Remembering to Say Thanks

Enter into his gates with thanksgiving, and into his courts
with praise: be thankful unto him, and bless his name.
For the LORD is good; his mercy is everlasting;
and his truth endureth to all generations.
Psalm 100:4–5 KJV

As a busy grandmom who takes responsibilities seriously, you will certainly find yourself caught up in the inevitable demands of everyday life. And when you do, it's only natural that you might, at times, fail to pause and thank your Creator for His blessings. But if the demands of grandparenting have caused you to take God's gifts for granted, it's time to rethink your habits and reorder your to-do list.

Whenever you slow down and express your sincere gratitude to the Father, you enrich your own life and the lives of your loved ones. So thanksgiving should become a habit, a regular part of your daily routine. God has blessed you beyond measure, and you owe Him everything, including your praise every day . . . starting now.

It is always possible to be thankful for what is given rather
than to complain about what is not given. One or the
other becomes a habit of life.
Elisabeth Elliot

Celebrating Life

Rejoice in the Lord always.
I will say it again: Rejoice!
Philippians 4:4 HCSB

Life is a cause for celebration, but sometimes we don't feel much like celebrating. In fact, when the weight of the world bears down upon our shoulders, celebration may be the last thing on our minds. But we need to remember that as God's children—and as the parents and grandparents of our own clans—we have been blessed beyond measure.

Remember this: today is a nonrenewable resource—once it's gone, it's gone forever. So celebrate the life God has given you by thinking optimistically about yourself, your family, and your future. Look up to the One who has showered you with blessings, and trust in your heart that He wants to give you so much more.

The highest and most desirable state of the soul
is to praise God in celebration for being alive.
Luci Swindoll

January 9

The Gift of Family

*These should learn first of all to put their religion into
practice by caring for their own family.*
1 Timothy 5:4 NIV

As every grandparent knows, family life is a mixture of conversations, mediations, irritations,
deliberations, commiserations, frustrations, negotia-
tions, and celebrations. In other words, the life of the
typical grandmom is incredibly varied.

Certainly, in the life of every family, there are
moments of frustration and disappointment. Lots of
them. But for those who are blessed to interact with
a close-knit, caring clan, the rewards far outweigh
the frustrations. That's why you pray fervently for
your family members, and that's why you love them
despite their faults.

Your clan is God's gift to you. That little band of
men, women, kids, and babies is a priceless treasure
on temporary loan from the Father above. Remember
to see your family as a gift . . . and act accordingly.

*Living life with a consistent spiritual walk deeply
influences those we love most.*
Vonette Bright

Faith for the Journey

Whatever is born of God overcomes the world.
And this is the victory that has overcome
the world—our faith.
1 John 5:4 NKJV

Are you a grandmother whose faith is evident for all to see? Hopefully so, because genuine faith is never meant to be locked up in the heart of a single person; it is meant to be shared. And a woman who wishes to share God's good news with the world should begin by sharing that message with her own family.

Every life—including yours—is a series of successes and failures, joys and sorrows, celebrations and disappointments. Every step of the way, through every triumph and tragedy, God offers you strength. Your challenge is to accept His gifts and remain faithful in every season of life.

Seeds of faith are always within us;
sometimes it takes a crisis to nourish
and encourage their growth.
Susan L. Taylor

Your Leadership Role

Those who are wise will shine as bright as the sky,
and those who turn many to righteousness
will shine like stars forever.
Daniel 12:3 NLT

Among your many important roles as a grandparent are those of mentor, advisor, and leader to your family. Your leadership is important to your loved ones and to your Creator. Why? Because you have many lessons to teach, both with your words and (more important) with your example.

If you'd like a leadership guidebook that never fails, you can probably find it on your bookshelf: it's God's Holy Word. When you make God's teachings your teachings, your loved ones will reap the benefits of your wisdom.

Our world needs responsible leaders and so does your family. So make this pledge and keep it: vow to be a godly example to your children and grandchildren. Your family needs you now, and you need the experience of leading them . . . now.

There is so much to teach,
and the time goes so fast.
Erma Bombeck

Don't Give Up!

If you do nothing in a difficult time,
your strength is limited.
Proverbs 24:10 HCSB

Occasional disappointments, detours, and failures are inevitable, even for the most accomplished among us. Setbacks are simply the price that we must sometimes pay for our willingness to take risks as we follow our dreams. But when we encounter these hardships, we must never lose faith.

Are you willing to keep fighting the good fight even when you meet unexpected difficulties? Hopefully so. If you decide to press on through temporary setbacks, you may soon be surprised at the creative ways God finds to help determined people, like you—people who possess wisdom and the courage to persevere.

Failure isn't falling down.
It's staying down.
Mary Pickford

The Power of a Positive Example

*Be an example to the believers in word, in conduct,
in love, in spirit, in faith, in purity.*
1 Timothy 4:12 NKJV

When you make yourself a living, breathing example of what it means to be a responsible human being, you give your children and grandchildren a gift that money simply cannot buy.

What lessons did you learn from your parents and grandparents? And what lessons are you passing on to the next two generations? These questions deserve to be answered *by you*. After all, our children and grandchildren learn best, not from the lessons we preach (with our words), but from the lessons we show them (with our actions).

The best time to share your wisdom—and the best time to be a positive role model—is now. And the best way to transfer wisdom from one generation to another is by making certain that the lessons you teach are clearly reinforced by the life you live.

*Life is not easy for any of us. But it is a continual
challenge, and it is up to us to be cheerful and to be
strong, so that those who depend on us may draw strength
from our example.*
Rose Kennedy

When It's Hard to Forgive and Forget

If you forgive people their wrongdoing, your heavenly Father will forgive you as well. But if you don't forgive people, your Father will not forgive your wrongdoing.
Matthew 6:14–15 HCSB

Life would be much simpler if you could forgive people "once and for all" and be done with it. Yet forgiveness is seldom that easy. Usually, the decision to forgive is straightforward, but the process of forgiving is more difficult, even for sensible grandmothers like you. Why? Because forgiveness is a journey that requires effort, time, perseverance, and prayer.

God instructs you to treat other people exactly as you wish to be treated. And since you want to be forgiven for the mistakes you make (no grandmother is perfect, not even you!), you must be willing to extend forgiveness to other people for the mistakes they have made. If you can't seem to forgive someone, you should keep asking God to help you until you can. And you can be sure of this: if you keep asking for God's help, He will give it.

Forgiveness is nothing compared to forgetting.
Bessie Delaney

MARY Stern Died
1/14/2010

Managing Change

The wise see danger ahead and avoid it,
but fools keep going and get into trouble.
Proverbs 27:12 NCV

There is no doubt about it: your world is changing constantly. Your circumstances are changing, your family is changing, and you are changing. So today's question for you, Grandmom, is this: How will you manage all those changes? Will you do your best and trust God with the rest, or will you spend fruitless hours worrying about things you can't control, while doing precious little else? The answer to these simple questions will help determine the direction of your day and the quality of your life.

The best way to confront change is head-on . . . and with God by your side. The same God who created the universe will protect you if you ask Him, so ask Him. When you do, you may rest assured that while the world changes moment by moment, God's love endures—unfathomable and unchanging—forever.

With God, it isn't who you were that matters;
it's who you are becoming.
Liz Curtis Higgs

The Gift of Love

Now faith, hope, love, abide these three;
but the greatest of these is love.
1 Corinthians 13:13 NASB

Love is a glorious gift from God; it's a gift that God shares with us, and it's a gift that He intends for us to share with others.

It has been said, and quite correctly so, that *grandmother* is simply another name for love. Grandmothers understand the power of love, and they share that message with the family. A grandmother shares her love through words and—more important— through deeds. The beneficiaries of that love are forever blessed.

A grandmother's love becomes her permanent legacy, her timeless gift to the family. It is a gift to her children, to her grandchildren, and to subsequent generations. It is her greatest gift and her most precious bequest.

Becoming a grandmother brings the satisfaction
of giving and receiving love, sometimes more generously
and more freely than ever before.
Sheila Kitzinger

Time for Fun

Sing a new song to him; play well and joyfully.
Psalm 33:3 NCV

Are you a grandmother who takes time each day to really enjoy life? Hopefully so. After all, you are the recipient of a precious gift—the gift of life. And because God has seen fit to give you this gift, it is incumbent upon you to use it and enjoy it. But sometimes, amid the inevitable pressures of everyday living, really enjoying life may seem almost impossible. It is not.

For most of us, fun is as much a function of attitude as it is a function of environment. So whether you're standing victorious atop one of life's mountains or trudging through one of life's valleys, enjoy yourself. You deserve to have fun today, and God wants you to have fun today . . . so what on earth are you waiting for?

A bonus of being a grandmother is
rediscovering the delights of play.
Sheila Kitzinger

Your Cheerful Heart

A cheerful heart is good medicine,
but a broken spirit saps a person's strength.
Proverbs 17:22 NLT

We must never underestimate the power of a grandmother's smile, a grandmother's kind word, or a grandmother's hug. And we must never underestimate the importance of cheerfulness. The Bible teaches us that a cheerful heart is like medicine: it makes us (and the people around us) feel better. So where does cheerfulness begin? Does it begin on the outside; is it a result of our possessions or our circumstances? Or does it begin on the inside, as a result of our attitudes?

The world would like you to believe that material possessions can create happiness, but you're too wise to be taken in by that. You know that lasting happiness can't be bought; it must be earned—earned with positive thoughts, heartfelt prayers, good deeds, and a cheerful heart . . . like yours.

We may run, walk, stumble, drive, or fly, but let us never
lose sight of the reason for the journey,
or miss a chance to see a rainbow on the way.
Gloria Gaither

Hugs Now

For the happy heart, life is a continual feast.
Proverbs 15:15 NLT

Dear Grandmother, do you know somebody who needs a hug (or a smile, or a kind word) right now? Maybe this person is related to you by birth, or maybe not. In either case, it's up to you to do something—not tomorrow, not next week—right now.

Of course your calendar is full. You may have many obligations, a full to-do list, and many people to care for. No matter. God's Word teaches you to share love today (not at some point in the future).

When it comes to planting God's seeds in the soil of eternity, the only certain time that we have is now. And when it comes to sharing hugs with our family and friends, there's simply no time like the present.

A silent hug means more than a thousands words
to a suffering heart.
Author Unknown

They Need Mentors

The lips of the righteous feed many.
Proverbs 10:21 HCSB

Your children and grandchildren need mentors—are you willing to be one? Hopefully so. The younger generation is faced with an ever-expanding array of challenges and temptations. The younger members of your family need your wisdom . . . and they need it now.

Even if your advice is sound, you can never be certain that it will be taken. Young people (like their older counterparts) can be remarkably hardheaded at times. Each generation, it appears, must learn anew the lessons of the last. Nonetheless, your words have an impact. So take time today to share your wisdom with the kids you love most . . . your own.

No matter how crazy or nutty your life has seemed,
God can make something strong and good out of it.
He can help you grow wide branches
for others to use as shelter.
Barbara Johnson

How Much Does God Love You?

The Lord is good, and His love is eternal;
His faithfulness endures through all generations.
Psalm 100:5 HCSB

How much does God love you and your family? More than you can comprehend. God's love is as vast as it is timeless; it is a boundless love that defies human understanding. Yet even though you cannot full understand God's love, you can respond to it.

Your loving heavenly Father never leaves you for an instant. In fact, He is with you right now, offering His protection and His strength. How will you respond to Him? Will you thank Him for His blessings, and will you praise Him for His gifts? I hope so. After all, the Creator deserves your thanks, and you deserve the experience of thanking Him.

So please don't wait until the fourth Thursday in November. Make every single day, including this one, a time of thanksgiving.

There is no pit so deep that God's love is not deeper still.
Corrie ten Boom

Give Thanks for Your Hard Work and Your Good Luck

Thanks be to God for His indescribable gift!
2 Corinthians 9:15 NKJV

It's an old idea and a true one: "The harder you work, the luckier you are." And as a grandmother, you certainly know a few things about both sides of that equation—you know quite a lot about work and just as much about luck . . . from firsthand experience. The fact that you're still on the job fulfilling your role as a responsible grandparent means you're probably working hard . . . and it also means you're incredibly fortunate to be the grandmother of your grandkids.

Your family is a unique blessing from the Creator, a gift that He expects you to cherish and care for. So, today, say a prayer of thanks for the job of being a grandparent. And as you think about your own personal mixture of hard work and good fortune, thank God for both.

*Every child's relationship with a close
and loving grandmother is unique.*
Arthur Kornhaber

Guard Your Heart

Guard your heart above all else, for it is the source of life.
Proverbs 4:23 HCSB

You are near and dear to God. He loves you (and yours) more than you can imagine, and He wants the very best for you (and yours). And one more thing, Grandmother: God wants you (and your clan) to guard your heart—but the world may tempt you to let down your guard.

The world has a way of capturing your attention and distorting your thoughts. Society wants you and your loved ones to focus on worldly matters. God, on the other hand, wants you to focus on Him.

Your task, of course, is to make sure that you focus your thoughts and energies on God's priorities, things that enrich your life and enhance your faith. So, today, be watchful and obedient. Guard your heart by giving it to your heavenly Father; it is safe with Him.

The health of anything—whether a garden plant
or a heart devoted to God—reflects what is going on (or not
going on!) underground.
Elizabeth George

Forgiveness Now

Hatred stirs up dissension, but love covers over all wrongs.
Proverbs 10:12 NIV

There's no doubt about it: forgiveness is difficult. Being frail, fallible, imperfect human beings, we are quick to anger, quick to blame, slow to forgive, and even slower to forget. Yet we are instructed to forgive others, just as we, too, have been forgiven.

How often must we forgive our family members and friends? More times than we can count. Our children (and their children) are precious but imperfect; so are our spouses and our friends. We must, on occasion, forgive those who have injured us; to do otherwise is to disobey God.

If there exists even one person, alive or dead, whom you have not forgiven (and that includes yourself), follow God's commandment and His will for your life: forgive. Hatred and bitterness and regret are not parts of God's plan for your life. Forgiveness is.

God calls upon the loved not just to love
but to be loving. God calls upon the forgiven
not just to forgive but to be forgiving.
Beth Moore

It's a Matter of Discipline

God hasn't invited us into a disorderly, unkempt life
but into something holy and beautiful—
as beautiful on the inside as the outside.

1 Thessalonians 4:7 MSG

Parents and grandparents who study the Bible are
confronted again and again with God's intention
that His children (of all ages) lead disciplined lives.
God doesn't reward laziness or misbehavior. To the
contrary, He expects His own to adopt a disciplined
approach to their lives. Yet we live in a world in which
leisure is often glorified and misbehavior is often
glamorized. We inhabit a society where sloppy is in
and neatness is out. We stand by and watch as the
media often puts bad behavior on a pedestal. But
God has other plans.

God did not create us for lives of mischief or
mediocrity; He created us for far greater things. So
wise parents (and their parents) teach discipline by
word and by example, but not necessarily in that
order.

Some people regard discipline as a chore.
For me, it is a kind of order that sets me free to fly.

Julie Andrews

The Wisdom to Be Humble

*Don't be selfish. . . . Be humble, thinking of others
as better than yourself.*

Philippians 2:3 TLB

Humility is not, in most cases, a naturally occurring human trait. Most of us, it seems, are more than willing to overestimate our own accomplishments. We are tempted to say, "Look how wonderful I am!" . . . hoping all the while that the world will agree with our own self-appraisals. But those of us who fall prey to the sin of pride should beware—God is definitely not impressed by our prideful proclamations.

As a savvy grandmother, you've already learned the value of humility. Now it's time to make sure your family learns it too. God still has some important lessons to teach your clan—lessons about humility that they may still need to learn. And the sooner you help them learn those lessons, the happier everybody will be.

*Humility is the root, mother, nurse, foundation, and bond
of all virtue.*

St. John Chrysostom

Living Purposefully

You're sons of Light, daughters of Day.
We live under wide open skies and know where we stand.
So let's not sleepwalk through life.
1 Thessalonians 5:5–6 MSG

Wise grandmothers understand that life is best lived on purpose. And purpose, like everything else in the universe, begins with God. Whether we realize it or not, God has a plan for each of us; He leads us in a direction of His choosing, but He won't force us to follow His path or His Son. It's up to each of us to make our own decisions about the way we choose to live our lives. When we welcome Him into our hearts and establish a genuine relationship with His Son, the Creator begins to make His purposes known.

Today, Grandmother, encourage your kids and grandkids to think carefully about the direction of their lives and the quality of their choices. After all, you know that your children (and their children) need a clear sense of purpose. Please make sure they know it too.

We set our eyes on the finish line, forgetting
the past, and straining toward the mark
of spiritual maturity and fruitfulness.
Vonette Bright

At Peace?

> *I leave you peace; my peace I give you.*
> *I do not give it to you as the world does.*
> *So don't let your hearts be troubled or afraid.*
>
> John 14:27 NCV

For on-the-go grandmothers, a moment's peace can be a scarce commodity. But no matter how numerous the interruptions and demands of the day, God is everpresent, always ready and willing to offer solace to those who seek "the peace that passes all understanding."

Have you found God's peace? Or are you still rushing after the illusion of "peace and happiness" that the world promises but cannot deliver? Today, as a gift to yourself, to your family, and to your friends, claim the inner peace that is your spiritual birthright: God's peace. It is a peace that passes all understanding, yet while you may not be able to comprehend it fully, you can still experience it frequently . . . and you should.

> *I want first of all . . . to be at peace with myself.*
> *I want a singleness of eye, a purity of intention,*
> *a central core to my life . . . I want, in fact—to borrow from*
> *the language of the saints—to live*
> *"in grace" as much of the time as possible.*
>
> Anne Morrow Lindbergh

Accepting God's Abundance

*I have come that they may have life,
and that they may have it more abundantly.*
John 10:10 NKJV

The tenth chapter of John tells us that Christ came to earth so that our lives might be filled with abundance. But what, exactly, did Jesus mean when He promised "life . . . more abundantly"? Was He referring to material possessions or financial wealth? Hardly. Jesus offers a different kind of abundance: a spiritual richness that extends beyond the temporal boundaries of this world.

Is material abundance part of God's plan for our lives? Perhaps. But in every circumstance of life, during times of wealth or times of want, God will provide us what we need if we trust Him. May we, as believers, claim the riches of Christ Jesus every day that we live, and may we share His blessings with all who cross our paths.

*God is the giver, and we are the receivers.
And His richest gifts are bestowed not upon those who
do the greatest things, but upon those who accept His
abundance and His grace.*
Hannah Whitall Smith

Taking Time to Teach

Fix these words of mine in your hearts and minds. . . .
Teach them to your children, talking about them
when you sit at home and when you walk along the road,
when you lie down and when you get up.

Deuteronomy 11:18–19 NIV

Daniel Webster wrote, "If we work in marble, it will perish; if we work upon brass, time will efface it; if we rear temples, they will crumble into dust; but if we work upon immortal minds and instill in them just principles, we are then engraving upon tablets which no time will efface, but which will brighten and brighten to all eternity." These words remind us of the glorious opportunities that are available to those of us who teach. And make no mistake, Grandmother, you can be, and should be, an important role model and teacher to your grandkids.

Being a parent or grandparent in today's difficult world requires insight, discipline, patience, and prayer. May you, with God's help, touch the hearts and minds of your grandchildren and, in doing so, refashion this wonderful world . . . and the next.

If you would civilize a man,
begin with his grandmother.

Victor Hugo

Laboring for the Harvest

I saw that the best thing people can do is to enjoy their work, because that is all they have. No one can help another person see what will happen in the future.

Ecclesiastes 3:22 NCV

Once the season for planting is upon us, the time to plant seeds is when we make time to plant seeds. And when it comes to planting God's seeds in the soil of eternity, the only certain time that we have is now. Yet because we are fallible human beings with limited vision and misplaced priorities, we may be tempted to delay.

If we hope to reap a bountiful harvest for God, for our families, and for ourselves, we must plant now by defeating a dreaded human frailty: the habit of procrastination. Procrastination often results from our shortsighted attempts to postpone temporary discomfort.

A far better strategy is this: Whatever "it" is, do it now. When you do, you won't have to worry about "it" later.

Rather than face the mere possibility of pain, we sometimes remain inactive, or we may do something easier than we should attempt. This is illogical, of course.

Dorothea Brande

February

Thank-You Hug for Grandmother

Dear Grandmother,

The very best mothers not only give life, but they also teach it. And that's exactly what you've done. For longer than we can remember, you've taught us life's most important lessons. You are our teacher, we are your pupils, and class is still in session.

One of life's great ironies is that there is so much to learn and so little time. That's why we value the lessons you have already taught us and the lessons you still have to teach.

Honoring God

Honor the LORD with your possessions,
and with the firstfruits of all your increase;
so your barns will be filled with plenty.

Proverbs 3:9–10 NKJV

Whom will you choose to honor today? If you honor God and place Him at the center of your life, every day is a cause for celebration. But if you fail to honor your heavenly Father, you're asking for trouble, and lots of it.

At times, your life may seem hectic, demanding, and complicated. And if the demands of life leave you rushing from place to place with scarcely a moment to spare, you may fail to pause and thank your Creator for the blessings He has bestowed upon you. But there's a better way.

So slow down and give God the time and praise He deserves. Honor Him for who He is and for what He has done for you. And don't just honor Him on Sunday morning. Praise Him every morning, including, of course, this one.

The greatest honor you can give almighty God
is to live gladly and joyfully because of
the knowledge of His love.

Julian of Norwich

Beyond Bitterness

*If you harbor bitter envy and selfish ambition in your
hearts, do not boast about it or deny the truth.
Such "wisdom" does not come down from heaven
but is earthly, unspiritual . . .*

James 3:14–15 NIV

Bitterness is a spiritual sickness. It will consume
your soul; it is dangerous to your emotional
health. It can destroy you if you let it . . . so don't
let it!

If you are caught up in intense feelings of anger
or resentment, you know all too well the destructive
power of these emotions. How can you rid yourself
of these feelings? First, you must prayerfully ask God
to cleanse your heart. Then, you must learn to catch
yourself whenever bitter thoughts return. You must
learn to resist negative thoughts before they hijack
your emotions.

When you learn to direct your thoughts toward
more positive (and rational) topics, you'll be protected
from the spiritual and emotional consequences of
bitterness . . . and you'll be wiser, healthier, and
happier too. So, Grandmother, why wait? Defeat
destructive bitterness today.

Bitterness is the trap that snares the hunter.

Max Lucado

God's Gift to You

*Everything God made is good, and nothing should be
refused if it is accepted with thanks.*

1 Timothy 4:4 NCV

Life is God's gift to you, and He intends that you celebrate His glorious gift. So when precisely will your celebration begin? If you're a thoughtful, God-fearing grandmother who treasures each day, the answer to that questions should be "as soon as possible, if not sooner!"

Folks who choose to fashion their days around God's love and God's promises are, quite literally, transformed: they see the world differently, they act differently, and they feel differently about themselves, their families, and their neighbors.

So whatever this day holds for you, begin it and end it with God as your partner. And throughout the day, give thanks to the One who created you. God's love for you is infinite. Accept it joyously, and be thankful.

*Your life is not a boring stretch of highway.
It's a straight line to heaven. And just look at the
fields ripening along the way. Look at the tenacity and
endurance. Look at the grains of righteousness. You'll have
quite a crop at harvest . . .
so don't give up!*

Joni Eareckson Tada

Leaving a Legacy of Wisdom

Choose my teachings instead of silver, and knowledge rather than the finest gold. Wisdom is more precious than rubies. Nothing you could want is equal to it.

Proverbs 8:10–11 NCV

Having given the gift of life, who better to explain it than grandmothers? The answer, of course, is nobody. So here are two questions for you to ponder today, Grandmother: First, what lessons are you teaching your grandkids? And second, what lasting legacy will you leave them when you are gone?

Our greatest gifts to future generations are not denominated in dollars, and our best bequests are not the material possessions we leave behind. Our greatest gifts are the timeless principles and enduring values we share (with our words) and demonstrate (with our deeds). So today and every day, think carefully about the things you stand for, and be sure to let your family know precisely where you stand. When you do, you'll be leaving a lasting legacy to your children, and to their children, and to generations yet unborn.

The role of teacher is one of the most important for any grandparent.

Arthur Kornhaber

The Best Day to Celebrate

Celebrate God all day, every day. I mean, revel in him!
Philippians 4:4 MSG

What is the best day to celebrate life? This one! Today and every day should be a day of prayer and celebration as you consider the joys and opportunities of loving and caring for your family.

What do you expect from the day ahead? Are you an optimistic grandmother who's expecting God to do wonderful things for you and yours, or are you living beneath a cloud of apprehension and doubt? The answer to this question will determine, to a surprising extent, the quality of your day and the quality of your family life.

So as you plan for the day ahead, remember that it's up to you to make sure that celebration is woven into the very fabric of your life. And if you can't find ways to celebrate your family, you're probably not paying attention.

If you can forgive the person you were,
accept the person you are, and believe in
the person you will become, you are headed for joy.
So celebrate your life.
Barbara Johnson

A Grandmother's Heart

Let love and faithfulness never leave you. . . .
Write them on the tablet of your heart.

Proverbs 3:3 NIV

Few things in life are as precious or as enduring as a grandmother's love. A grandmother's love is powerful and priceless.

The familiar words of 1 Corinthians 13 remind us that faith is important, as is hope. But love is more important still.

Jesus showed His love for us on the cross, and we are called to return His love by sharing it. We are instructed to love one another just as Christ loved us.

Sometimes love is easy (puppies and sleeping children come to mind) and sometimes love is hard (fallible human beings come to mind). But God's Word is clear: We are to love our families and our neighbors without reservation or condition. No exceptions.

How do you spell love? When you reach the point where
the happiness, security, and development of another person
is as much of a driving force to you as your own happiness,
security, and development, then you have a mature love.
True love is spelled G-I-V-E.
It is not based on what you can get,
but rooted in what you can give to the other person.

Josh McDowell

Unshaken

*Those who trust in the LORD are like Mount Zion.
It cannot be shaken; it remains forever.*
Psalm 125:1 HCSB

Sometimes our most important journeys are the ones that we take to the winding conclusion of what seem to be dead-end streets. Thankfully, with God there are no dead ends; there are only opportunities to learn, to yield, to trust, to serve, and to grow.

The next time you experience one of life's inevitable disappointments, don't despair, and don't be afraid to try Plan B. Consider every setback an opportunity to choose a different, more appropriate path. Have faith that God may indeed be leading you in an entirely different direction, a direction of His choosing. Build your future on the rock that cannot be shaken. And as you take your next step, Grandmother, remember that what looks like a dead end may, in fact, be the fast lane according to God.

The Lord God of heaven and earth, the Almighty Creator of all things, He who holds the universe in His hand as though it were a very little thing, He is your Shepherd, and He has charged Himself with the care and keeping of you, as a shepherd is charged with the care and keeping of his sheep.
Hannah Whitall Smith

February 8

Giving It Your Best

Even a child is known by his doings,
whether his work be pure, and whether it be right.
Proverbs 20:11 KJV

How does God intend for us to work? Does He intend for us to work diligently, or does He, instead, reward mediocrity? The answer is obvious. God has created a world in which hard work is rewarded and sloppy work is not. Yet sometimes we may seek ease over excellence, or we may be tempted to take shortcuts, when God intends that we walk the straight-and-narrow path.

Today, Grandmother, give your best, and encourage your loved ones to do likewise. Wherever you find yourself, whether at home, at church, in the workplace, or just about any place in between, do your work, and do it with all your heart. You'll be a marvelous example to your children and grandchildren. But more important, God will bless your efforts and use you in ways that only He can understand. So do your job with focus and dedication. And leave the rest up to God.

Excellence is not perfection, but essentially a desire to be
strong in the Lord and for the Lord.
Cynthia Heald

Praying for Our Children

*Do not be anxious about anything, but in everything, by
prayer and petition, with thanksgiving,
present your requests to God.*

Philippians 4:6 NIV

Every child is different, but every child is similar
in this respect: he or she is a priceless gift from
the Father above. And with the Father's gift comes
immense responsibilities.

Our children are not perfect (who is?), but they
are blessings from above. And as responsible parents
and grandparents, we must create homes in which
the future generation can grow and flourish.

Today, let us pray for our children . . . all of them.
Let us pray for children here at home and for children
around the world. Every child is God's child. May we,
as concerned adults, behave—and pray—accordingly.

*Praying for our children is a noble task.
There is nothing more special, more precious,
than time that a parent spends struggling and pondering
with God on behalf of a child.*

Max Lucado

Above and Beyond Discouragement

*He gives strength to the weary
and strengthens the powerless.*
Isaiah 40:29 HCSB

When we fail to meet the expectations of others (or, for that matter, the expectations that we have set for ourselves), we may be tempted to abandon hope. Thankfully, on those cloudy days when our strength is sapped and our faith is shaken, there exists a source from which we can draw courage and wisdom.

You live in a world where expectations can be high and demands can be even higher. The pressures of everyday life can be stifling, and it's no surprise you can become discouraged . . . but you need not stay discouraged.

If you become disheartened by the direction of your day or your life, turn your thoughts and prayers to God, and He will respond. He will help you count your blessings instead of your hardships. And then with a renewed spirit of optimism and hope, you can properly thank your Father in heaven for His gifts by using them.

*The most profane word we use is "hopeless."
When you say a situation or person is hopeless,
you are slamming the door in the face of God.*
Kathy Troccoli

When Times Are Tough

*Be of good courage, and he shall strengthen your heart,
all ye that hope in the LORD.*
Psalm 31:24 KJV

When tough times arrive, we have a clear choice: we can begin the difficult work of tackling our troubles . . . or not. When we summon the courage to look Old Man Trouble squarely in the eye, he usually blinks. But if we refuse to address our problems, even the smallest annoyances have a way of growing into king-sized catastrophes.

Are you anxious? Take those anxieties to God. Are you troubled? Take your troubles to Him. Does the world seem to be trembling beneath your feet? Seek protection from the One who cannot be moved.

The same God who created the universe stands ready and willing to comfort you and to restore your strength. During life's most difficult days, your heavenly Father remains steadfast. And in His own time and according to His master plan, He will heal you if you invite Him into your heart.

*Without the burden of afflictions,
it is impossible to reach the height of grace.
The gift of grace increases as the struggles increase.*
St. Rose of Lima

More to Learn Every Day

There's something here also for seasoned men and women,
still a thing or two for the experienced to learn—
Fresh wisdom to probe and penetrate, the rhymes and
reasons of wise men and women. Start with God.

Proverbs 1:5–7 MSG

Even if you're a very savvy grandmother, God isn't finished with you yet, and He isn't finished teaching you important lessons about life here on earth and life eternal.

As a spiritual being, you have the potential to grow in your personal knowledge of the Lord every day that you live. You can do so through prayer, through worship, through an openness to God, and through a careful study of His Holy Word. Your Bible contains powerful prescriptions for everyday living. If you sincerely seek to walk with God, you should commit yourself to the thoughtful study of His teachings.

When you study God's Word and follow in the footsteps of His Son, you will become wise . . . and you will serve as a shining example to your friends, to your family, and to the world.

Today is yesterday's pupil.

Thomas Fuller

Surviving Life's Storms

He said to them, "Why are you fearful,
O you of little faith?" Then He arose and rebuked
the winds and the sea, and there was a great calm.

Matthew 8:26 NKJV

A frightening storm rose quickly on the Sea of Galilee, and the disciples were afraid. Because of their limited faith, they feared for their lives. When they turned to Jesus, He calmed the waters, and He rebuked His disciples for their lack of faith in Him.

On occasion, we, like the disciples, are frightened by the inevitable storms of life. Why are we afraid? Because we, like the disciples, possess imperfect faith.

When we genuinely accept God's promises as absolute truth, when we trust Him with life here on earth and life eternal, we have little to fear. Faith, then, serves as a powerful antidote to worry, a source of courage and strength for ourselves and our families. So today, Grandmother, take your fears to God and leave them there. Permanently.

His hand on me is a father's hand, gently guiding and
encouraging. His hand lets me know
he is with me, so I am not afraid.

Mary Morrison Suggs

Let's Laugh

Clap your hands, all you nations;
shout to God with cries of joy.
Psalm 47:1 NIV

Family life is serious business—it should be taken very seriously . . . up to a point. But no grandmother's responsibilities should be so burdensome that she forgoes her daily quota of chuckles, snickers, and guffaws. So please don't forget to laugh.

You don't have to be a stand-up comedienne to see the humorous side of life, and you don't have to memorize a string of one-liners in order to enjoy good clean humor. Humor tends to come naturally when you enjoy healthy relationships. Plus, you're more likely to laugh if you don't take yourself too seriously.

So today, as you go about your daily activities, approach your relationships and your life with a smile on your lips and a chuckle in your heart. After all, God created laughter for a reason . . . and Father indeed knows best. So laugh!

He who laughs lasts—he who doesn't, doesn't.
Author Unknown

The Joy He Has Promised

Now I am coming to You, and I speak these things in the world so that they may have My joy completed in them.
John 17:13 HCSB

God intends that we should share His joy. In fact, the Bible teaches us that God's plan for our lives includes great joy, but our heavenly Father will not compel us to be joyful. We have to accept His joy (or reject it) ourselves.

Sometimes amid the inevitable hustle and bustle of life here on earth, we can forfeit—at least for a while—God's peace as we struggle along the uphill climb that, for most of us, constitutes the pilgrimage through and beyond the challenges of everyday life. That pilgrimage is seldom easy, but with God as our traveling companion, we can always find strength for the journey.

So, Grandmother, here's a prescription for better spiritual health: learn to trust God, and open the door of your soul to Him. When you do, He will most certainly give you the peace and the joy He has promised.

It is the definition of joy to be able to offer back to God the essence of what he's placed in you, be that creativity or a love of ideas or a compassionate heart or the gift of hospitality.
Paula Rinehart

Looking for People to Help

Whenever you are able, do good to people who need help.
Proverbs 3:27 NCV

Neighbors. We know that we are instructed to love them, and yet there's so little time . . . and we're so busy.

In order to love our neighbors as God intends, we must first slow down long enough to understand their needs. Slowing down, however, is not as simple as it seems. We live in a fast-paced world with pressures and demands that often sap our time and our energy. Sometimes we may convince ourselves that slowing down is not an option, but we are wrong. Caring for our neighbors must be our priority because it is God's priority.

This very day, you will encounter someone who needs a word of encouragement or a pat on the back or a helping hand or a heartfelt prayer. And if you don't reach out to that person, who will?

It is one of the most beautiful compensations of life that no one can sincerely try to help another without helping herself.
Barbara Johnson

Your Helping Hands

*Do not withhold good from those who deserve it
when it's in your power to help them.*

Proverbs 3:27 NLT

We live in a world that is, on occasion, a frightening place. Sometimes we sustain life-altering losses that are so profound and so tragic that it seems we might never recover. But with God's help and with the help of encouraging family members and friends, we can recover.

In times of need, God's Word is clear: we must offer comfort to those in need by sharing not only our courage but also our faith.

Do you know someone who needs a helping hand or an encouraging word? Of course you do. And the very best day to extend your helping hand is this one. So as you make your plans for the day ahead, look for somebody to help. When you do, you'll be a grandmother who's a powerful example to your family and a worthy servant to your Creator.

*So often we think that to be encouragers we have
to produce great words of wisdom when, in fact,
a few simple syllables of sympathy and an arm around the
shoulder can often provide
much needed comfort.*

Florence Littauer

Miracles at Your House

Is anything too hard for the LORD?
Genesis 18:14 NKJV

We human beings have a strange disinclination to believe in things that are beyond our meager abilities to understand. We read of God's miraculous works in biblical times, but we tell ourselves, "That was then, and this is now." When we do so, we are mistaken. Miracles—both great and small—happen around us all day every day, but usually we're too busy to notice. Some miracles, like the twinkling of a star or the glory of a sunset, we take for granted. Other miracles, like the healing of a terminally sick patient, we chalk up to fate or to luck. We assume, quite incorrectly, that God is "out there" and we are "right here." Nothing could be farther from the truth.

Today, trust God—His power and His miracles. And then, Grandmother, please wait patiently . . . something miraculous is about to happen.

For every mountain there is a miracle.
Robert Schuller

He Helps Us Endure

Patient endurance is what you need now,
so you will continue to do God's will.
Then you will receive all that he has promised.

Hebrews 10:36 NLT

If you've led a perfect life with absolutely no foul-ups, blunders, mistakes, or flops—and if your kids and grandkids have done likewise—you can skip this day's devotional. But if you're like the rest of us, you know that occasional disappointments and failures are an inevitable part of life. Such setbacks are simply the price we must pay for growing and learning.

When we encounter the inevitable difficulties of life here on earth, God stands ready to protect us. God promises that He is never distant and that He is always prepared to guide us and protect us when we ask Him. And while we are waiting for God's plans to unfold, we can be comforted in the knowledge that our Creator can overcome any obstacle, even if we cannot.

God does not promise to keep us out of the storms and
floods, but He does promise to sustain us in
the storm, and then bring us out in due time for
His glory when the storm has done its work.

Warren Wiersbe

Busy with Your Thoughts

*People's thoughts can be like a deep well, but someone
with understanding can find the wisdom there.*
Proverbs 20:5 NCV

Because we are human, we are always busy with our
thoughts. We simply can't help ourselves. Our
brains never shut off, and even while we're sleeping,
we mull things over in our subconscious minds. The
question is not will we think; the question is how will
we think and what will we think about.

Today, focus your thoughts on God's plan and
God's love. And if you've been plagued by pessimism
and doubt, it's time to rethink the way you've been
thinking!

So do yourself and your loved ones a big favor:
think optimistically about your world, your family,
and your life. It's the wise way to use your mind.
And besides, since you will always be busy with your
thoughts, you might as well make those thoughts
pleasing (to God) and helpful (to you and yours).

*I became aware of one very important concept I had
missed before: my attitude–not my circumstances–was
what was making me unhappy.*
Vonette Bright

Enough Rest?

I said to myself, "Relax and rest.
God has showered you with blessings."
Psalm 116:7 MSG

Physical exhaustion is God's way of telling us to slow down. God expects us to work hard, of course, but He also intends for us to rest. When we fail to take the rest that we need, we do a disservice to ourselves and to our families.

We live in a world that tempts us to stay up late—very late. But too much late-night TV, combined with too little sleep, is a prescription for exhaustion.

Are your physical or spiritual batteries running low? Is your energy on the wane? Are your emotions frayed? Because you're a loving grandmother who cares deeply for her family, you should take care of yourself so that you can truly take care of them. And taking care of yourself means getting enough rest. So tonight, at a sensible hour, turn your thoughts and your prayers to God. And when you're finished, turn off the lights and go to bed!

Life is strenuous.
See that your clock does not run down.
Mrs. Charles E. Cowman

Don't Stop Asking

*Keep asking, and it will be given to you. Keep searching,
and you will find. Keep knocking, and the door will be
opened to you. For everyone who asks receives,
and the one who searches finds, and to the one who
knocks, the door will be opened.*

Matthew 7:7–8 HCSB

Okay, Grandmother, here's a worthwhile question: How often do you ask God for His guidance and His wisdom? Occasionally? Intermittently? Whenever you experience a crisis? Hopefully not. Hopefully, you've acquired the habit of asking for God's assistance early and often. And hopefully, you have learned to seek His guidance in every aspect of your life.

God has promised that when you ask for His help, He will not withhold it. So ask. Ask Him to meet the needs of your day. Ask Him to lead you, to protect you, and to correct you. And trust the answers He gives.

God stands at the door and waits. When you knock, He opens. When you ask, He answers. Your task, of course, is to seek His guidance prayerfully, confidently, and often.

*When you ask God to do something,
don't ask timidly; put your whole heart into it.*

Marie T. Freeman

New Beginnings

There is a time for everything,
and a season for every activity under heaven.
Ecclesiastes 3:1 NIV

Each new day offers countless opportunities to serve God, to seek His will, and to follow His path, yet sometimes we wander aimlessly in a wilderness of our own making. Thankfully, we need never stay lost for long, because God has better plans of us. And whenever we ask Him to renew our strength and guide our steps, He does so.

So, Grandmom, consider this day a new beginning. Consider it a fresh start, a renewed opportunity to serve your Creator and your family with willing hands and a loving heart. Ask God to renew your sense of purpose as He guides your steps. Today is a glorious opportunity to serve God. Seize that opportunity while you can; tomorrow may indeed be too late.

More often than not, when something looks like
it's the absolute end, it is really the beginning.
Charles Swindoll

How to Recharge Your Batteries

Your Father knows what you need before you ask Him.
Matthew 6:8 NASB

Could you use a little extra energy? Or a lot? If so, you're not alone. All of us need to recharge our batteries from time to time, and you're no exception. But here's a word of warning: if you need more energy, don't make a beeline for the medicine cabinet or the espresso bar, because you'll never find lasting strength in a pill bottle or a cup of java. If you're looking for strength that lasts, the best place to start is with God.

Are you (or one of your family members) living under a cloud of uncertainty? If so, ask God where He wants you to go, and then go there.

In all matters, ask for God's guidance, and avail yourself of His power. When you do, you can be certain that He hears your prayers . . . and you can be certain that He will answer.

When the dream of our heart is one that God has planted there, a strange happiness flows into us.
At that moment, all of the spiritual resources of the universe are released to help us. Our praying is then at one with the will of God and becomes a channel for the Creator's purposes for us and our world.
Catherine Marshall

Actions Speak Louder

Be ye doers of the word, and not hearers only,
deceiving your own selves.

James 1:22 KJV

Are you a determined grandmom, a woman who is determined to make a difference in the lives of your family and friends? If so, you must make sure that your actions speak for themselves.

The old saying is both familiar and true: actions indeed speak louder than words. So as a thoughtful grandparent and a lifelong role model to your grandkids, it's up to you to make certain that your actions always speak well of your life and your legacy.

Sometimes you will be tempted to talk much and do less—you will be tempted to verbalize your beliefs rather than live by them. But it is never enough to wait idly by while others do the right thing; you, too, must act—starting now and ending never.

You may be disappointed if you fail,
but you are doomed if you don't try.

Beverly Sills

Swamped by Your Possessions?

Don't be obsessed with getting more material things.
Be relaxed with what you have.

Hebrews 13:5 MSG

Do you sometimes feel swamped by your possessions? Do you seem to be spending more and more time keeping track of the things you own while making mental notes of the things you intend to buy? If so, Grandmother, here's a word of caution: your fondness for material possessions may be getting in the way of your relationships—your relationships with the people around you and your relationship with God.

Society teaches us to honor possessions, but God teaches us to honor people—no if's, ands, or buts.

We must never invest too much energy in the acquisition of stuff. Earthly riches are here today and all too soon gone. Our real riches, of course, are in heaven, and that's where we should focus our thoughts and our energy.

It is not wrong to own things,
but it is wrong for things to own us.
Warren Wiersbe

Waiting Patiently for God

A patient person shows great understanding.
Proverbs 14:2 HCSB

The dictionary defines the word *patience* as "the ability to be calm, tolerant, and understanding." And for most of us, patience is a hard thing to master. Why? Because we have lots of things we want, and we know precisely when we want them: NOW (if not sooner). But the Bible teaches that we must learn to wait patiently for the things that God has in store for us, even when waiting is difficult.

We live in an imperfect world inhabited by imperfect people. Sometimes we inherit troubles from others, and sometimes we create troubles for ourselves. On other occasions we see people moving ahead in the world, and we want to move ahead with them. So we become impatient with ourselves, with our circumstances, and even with our Creator.

So, Grandmother, please do yourself this favor: be still before your heavenly Father, and trust His timetable. It's the peaceful way to live.

No matter what we are going through,
no matter how long the waiting for answers,
of one thing we may be sure. God is faithful.
He keeps His promises. What He starts,
He finishes . . . including His perfect work in us.
Gloria Gaither

How Will You Worship Today?

It is written, "You shall worship the LORD your God,
and Him only you shall serve."
Matthew 4:10 NKJV

All of mankind is engaged in the practice of
worship. Some choose to worship God and, as a
result, reap the joy that He intends for His children.
Others distance themselves from God by worshiping
such things as earthly possessions or personal
gratification . . . and when they do so, they suffer.

Today, Grandmother, as one way of worshiping
God, make every aspect of your life a cause for
celebration and praise. Praise God for the blessings
and opportunities that He has given you. God
deserves your worship, your prayers, your praise, and
your thanks. And you deserve the joy that is yours
when you worship Him with your prayers, with your
deeds, and with your life.

When you use your life for God's glory,
everything you do can become
an act of worship.
Rick Warren

March

Thank-You Hug for Grandmother

Dear Grandmother,

Thanks for your encouragement. Even when we did not believe in ourselves, you believed in us . . . and it showed.

You never gave up on us, and you never stopped believing in our abilities. Your faith eventually rubbed off on us: because you believe in us, we can believe in ourselves. And that, Grandmother, is the power of encouragement.

When The Storms of Life Rage

Jesus replied, "You of little faith, why are you so afraid?"
Then he got up and rebuked the winds and the waves,
and it was completely calm.
Matthew 8:26 NIV

As every grandmother knows, some days are just plain difficult.

When we find ourselves overtaken by the inevitable frustrations of life, we must catch ourselves, take a deep breath, and lift our thoughts upward. Although we are here on earth struggling to rise above the distractions of the day, we need never struggle alone. God is always with us; He is eternal and faithful.

If you find yourself enduring difficult circumstances, remember that God remains in His heaven. If you become discouraged with the direction of your day or your life, take a moment to offer your thoughts and prayers to Him. He is a God of possibility, not negativity. He will guide you through your difficulties and beyond them—beginning right now—if you ask.

When life is difficult, God wants us to have
a faith that trusts and waits.
Kay Arthur

The Seeds of Happiness

If they serve Him obediently, they will end their days in prosperity and their years in happiness.
Job 36:11 HCSB

Before she became America's first First Lady, Martha Washington had experienced the grief of losing her first husband. Yet despite the tragedies that she endured, Martha never allowed pessimism or doubt to cloud her vision. She said, "We carry the seeds of happiness with us wherever we go." And of course she was right.

So the next time you're feeling troubled, fearful, apathetic, or blue, remember that wherever you go, you carry within you the potential to be happy. Realizing that potential is up to you, but it's always there. So says the woman who was the mother of our country and the grandmother of seven lovely children. And as you're acutely aware, Grandmother always knows best.

Many persons have a wrong idea of what constitutes true happiness. It is not attained through self-gratification, but through fidelity to a worthy purpose.
Helen Keller

The Rewards of Integrity

*The integrity of the upright guides them,
but the unfaithful are destroyed by their duplicity.*
Proverbs 11:3 NIV

Grandmothers know, and the Bible makes it clear, that God rewards integrity just as surely as He punishes dishonesty. So if we seek to earn the kind of lasting rewards that God bestows upon those who obey His commandments, we must make honesty the hallmark of our dealings with others.

Character is built slowly over a lifetime. Character is the sum of every right decision, every honest word, every noble thought, and every heartfelt prayer. It is built upon a foundation of industry, generosity, and humility. Character is a precious thing—difficult to build but easy to tear down. As a caring grandparent, you must seek to live each day with discipline, honesty, and faith. When you do, integrity becomes a habit. And God smiles.

*Each one of us is God's special work of art.
Through us, He teaches and inspires, delights
and encourages, informs and uplifts all those who view our
lives. God, the master artist,
is most concerned about expressing Himself—
His thoughts and His intentions—through what
He paints in our characters.*
Joni Eareckson Tada

March 4

Beyond Doubt

Jesus said, "Don't let your hearts be troubled.
Trust in God, and trust in me."
John 14:1 NCV

If you've never had any doubts about your faith, then you can stop reading this page now and skip to the next. But if you've ever been plagued by doubts about your faith or your God, keep reading.

Even some of the most faithful women are, at times, tested by occasional bouts of discouragement and doubt. But even when you feel far removed from God, God is never far removed from you. He is always with us, always willing to calm the storms of life—always willing to replace your doubts with comfort and assurance.

Whenever you're plagued by doubts, that's precisely the moment you should seek God's presence by genuinely seeking to establish a deeper, more meaningful relationship with Him. Then, Grandmother, you may rest assured that, in time, God will calm your fears, answer your prayers, and restore your confidence.

We must lay our questions, frustrations, anxieties, and
impotence at the feet of God and wait for His answer.
And then receiving it, we must live by faith.
Kay Arthur

March 5

Precious Memories

I thank my God upon every remembrance of you.
Philippians 1:3 NKJV

Family memories: oh, how we treasure them. So it's no wonder we sometimes find ourselves reflecting fondly, if somewhat wistfully, on the past.

Grandparents are, and always have been, our family historians. Now, Grandmother, the history lessons are up to you. Your kids and their kids can learn much from you. Between your ears, you have a rich storehouse of lessons, traditions, parables, and biographies. And since there's no time like the present to share your insights, why not start sharing them today?

Because you're a wise woman with a thorough understanding of your family's history, you have stories to tell and memories to share with future generations. And if you don't share them, who else will? Who else can?

A grandparent's memories, those tales of times past, that seasoned view of the world—these are priceless gifts which the grandparent can offer to grandchildren.
Arthur Kornhaber

Slowing Down for God

Lead a quiet and peaceable life in all
godliness and honesty.
1 Timothy 2:2 KJV

If you're a grandparent with too many responsibilities and too few hours in which to fulfill them, you are not alone. Life is so demanding that sometimes you may feel as if you have no time for yourself . . . and no time for God.

Has the busy pace of life robbed you of the peace that can and should be yours? If so, you are simply too busy for your own good, and it's high time you did something about it. Thankfully, God is always available to you; your challenge, of course, is to make yourself available to Him.

Today, as a gift to yourself, to your family, and to the world, slow down long enough to claim the inner peace that is your spiritual birthright. It is offered freely; it has been paid for in full; it is yours for the asking. So ask. And then share.

Getting things accomplished isn't nearly as important as taking time for love.
Janette Oke

When Grief Visits

*Blessed are you who are hungry now,
because you will be filled. Blessed are you who weep now,
because you will laugh.*

Luke 6:21 HCSB

Grief visits all of us who live long and love deeply. When we lose a loved one, or when we experience any other profound loss, darkness overwhelms us for a while, and it seems as if we cannot summon the strength to face another day—but, with God's help, we can.

Thankfully, God promises that He is "close to the brokenhearted" (Psalm 34:18 NIV). In times of intense sadness, we can turn to Him, and we can turn to close friends and family. When we do, we can be comforted . . . and in time we will be healed.

Concentration-camp survivor Corrie ten Boom noted, "There is no pit so deep that God's love is not deeper still." Let us remember those words and live by them . . . especially when the days seem dark.

*Our tears do not fall without the hand of God catching
every one.*
Kathy Troccoli

Time for Silence

Be silent before Me.
Isaiah 41:1 HCSB

For busy women, each day can quickly be filled up with a wide assortment of responsibilities, distractions, interruptions, and commitments. And as a modern grandmom living in a clamorous society, you're not exempt from the stress and the noise. Yet the noisier your world becomes, the more you need to carve out meaningful moments for silence and meditation.

God isn't a skywriter; He doesn't spread His instructions across the morning sky for all to see. To the contrary, God often speaks in a still, quiet voice, a voice that can be drowned out by the noise of the day.

So even if your appointment book is filled from cover to cover, make time for silence. You should always have at least one serious chat with your Creator every day. He deserves it . . . and so do you.

*Deepest communion with God is beyond words,
on the other side of silence.*
Madeleine L'Engle

What Are You Doing with Your Talents?

*God has given gifts to each of you from his great variety
of spiritual gifts. Manage them well so that
God's generosity can flow through you.*
1 Peter 4:10 NLT

Your talents are special gifts from God. And the same applies to your children and grandchildren—their talents, too, are blessings from above, blessings that must be nurtured or forfeited.

God intends that we cultivate our talents and use them to improve our own lives and the lives of our neighbors. But if we overlook opportunities to grow or opportunities to serve, everybody loses.

Are you a grandmom who continues to maximize the talents God has given you? And are you encouraging your family members to do likewise? If so, keep up the good work. If not, remember this: the best way to say thank you for God's gifts is to use them.

*When I stand before God at the end of my life,
I would hope that I would not have a single bit
of talent left and could say,
"I used everything you gave me."*
Erma Bombeck

March 10

Lighting Your Path
with God's Word

Your word is a lamp to my feet and a light to my path.
Psalm 119:105 NASB

God has given us a guidebook for life; it's called the Holy Bible, and it contains thorough instructions which, when followed, lead to fulfillment, righteousness, and eternal life. Wise grandparents, being the experienced members of their families, bear a special responsibility to help their kids and grandkids understand the importance of biblical instruction.

The psalmist describes God's Word as, "a light to my path." Is the Bible your lamp? And your family's lamp too? Hopefully so, because God's Word never goes out of style, and it never grows stale. It can be a light to guide your steps. Claim it as your light today, tomorrow, and every day of your life—and then walk confidently in the footsteps of God's only begotten Son.

There is no way to draw closer to God unless you are in the Word of God every day.
It's your compass. Your guide. You can't get where you need to go without it.
Stormie Omartian

Old-Fashioned Courtesy
Still Matters

Be hospitable to one another without grumbling.
1 Peter 4:9 NKJV

As a woman who has experienced her fair share of life, you remember times when courtesy really mattered. Well, it still does. Of course, here in the twenty-first century, it sometimes seems like common courtesy is a decidedly uncommon trait. But if we are to trust the Bible—and we should—then we understand that kindness and courtesy will never go out of style. Your challenge, as a thoughtful grandmother and as a mentor to your friends and family, is to make sure that courtesy and kindness never go out of style at your house.

Today, make sure that you and yours offer the gift of courtesy to family members, to friends, and even to total strangers. Be gentle, considerate, and well mannered. And as you consider all the things that God has done for you, honor Him with your words and with your deeds. He expects no less; He deserves no less; and neither do the folks who cross your path.

Only the courteous can love,
but it is love that makes them courteous.
C. S. Lewis

How to Start Your Day

*Every morning he wakes me. He teaches me to listen
like a student. The Lord God helps me learn.*
Isaiah 50:4–5 NCV

Each new day is a gift from God, and wise
grandmoms spend a few quiet moments each
morning thanking the Giver. Daily life is woven with
the threads of habit, and no habit is more important
to our spiritual health than the discipline of daily
prayer and devotion to the Creator.

When we begin each day with our heads bowed
and our hearts lifted, we remind ourselves of God's
love, His protection, and His commandments. And if
we are wise, we align our priorities for the coming day
with the teachings and commandments that God has
given us through His Holy Word.

Are you seeking to change some aspect of your
life? Then take time out of your hectic schedule
to spend time each day with your Creator. Do you
seek to improve the condition of your spiritual or
physical health? If so, ask for God's help, and ask for
it many times each day . . . starting with your morning
devotional.

*We all need to make time for God.
Even Jesus made time to be alone with the Father.*
Kay Arthur

Never Lose Hope

Full of hope, you'll relax, confident again;
you'll look around, sit back, and take it easy.
Job 11:18 MSG

Are you a hope-filled grandparent? You should be. After all, God is good; His love endures; and He has blessed you with a loving family. But sometimes, in life's darker moments, you may lose sight of those blessings, and when you do, it's easy to lose hope.

If hope ever becomes a scarce commodity around your house, or if you find yourself falling into the spiritual traps of worry and discouragement, turn your concerns over to God in prayer. Then, seek wisdom and encouragement from trusted friends and family members. And remember this: the world can be a place of trials and tribulations, but God's love conquers all; He has promised you peace, joy, and eternal life. And, of course, God keeps His promises today, tomorrow, and forever, amen!

Teach us to set our hopes on heaven,
to hold firmly to the promise of eternal life,
so that we can withstand the struggles
and storms of this world.
Max Lucado

Respect Yourself

*You have made him a little lower than the angels,
and You have crowned him with glory and honor.*

Psalm 8:5 NKJV

Do you place a high value on your talents, your time, your capabilities, and your opportunities? If so, congratulations. But if you've acquired the insidious habit of devaluing your time, your work, or yourself, it's now time for a change. So, Grandmother, if you've unintentionally been squandering opportunities or somehow selling yourself short, please do yourself and your loved ones a favor by rethinking the way you think about yourself (got that?).

No one can live for you, and no one can build up your self-confidence if you're unwilling to believe in yourself. So if you've been talking disrespectfully to yourself, stop; if you've been underestimating your talents, cease. You deserve better treatment from yourself . . . far better. And if you don't give yourself healthy respect, who will?

As you and I lay up for ourselves living, lasting treasures in Heaven, we come to the awesome conclusion that we ourselves are His treasure!

Anne Graham Lotz

Joyful, Joyful!

How happy are those who can live in your house,
always singing your praises.
Happy are those who are strong in the LORD.
Psalm 84:4–5 NLT

A re you a grandparent whose joy is evident for all to see? If so, congratulations: your joyful spirit serves as a powerful example to your family. And because of your attitude, you may be assured that your children and grandchildren will be blessed by your enthusiasm.

Of course, sometimes amid the inevitable hustle and bustle of life here on earth, even the most optimistic among us can forfeit—albeit temporarily—the joy that God intends for us to experience. But with prayer and perspective, we can regain our bearings and reclaim our hopes.

God's plan for you and your family includes heaping helpings of abundance and joy. Claim them. And remember that Christ offers you and your family priceless gifts: His abundance, His peace, and His joy. Accept those gifts and share them freely, just as Christ has freely shared Himself with you.

Our God is so wonderfully good, and lovely, and blessed in
every way that the mere fact of belonging to Him is enough
for an untellable fullness of joy!
Hannah Whitall Smith

The Foundations of Family Ties and Friendships

Putting away lying, "Let each one of you speak truth with his neighbor," for we are members of one another.

Ephesians 4:25 NKJV

Family ties and lasting friendships are built upon a foundation of honesty and trust. It has been said on many occasions that honesty is the best policy. Yet it is far more important to note that honesty is God's policy.

Sometimes honesty is difficult; sometimes honesty is painful; sometimes honesty makes us feel uncomfortable. Despite these temporary feelings of discomfort, we must make honesty the hallmark of all our relationships; otherwise, we invite needless suffering into our own lives and into the lives of those we love.

Sometime soon, perhaps even today, you will be tempted to bend the truth. Resist that temptation. Truth is God's way. Always make it your way too.

The single most important element in any human relationship is honesty—with oneself, with God, and with others.

Catherine Marshall

A Storehouse of Knowledge

The wise store up knowledge.
Proverbs 10:14 HCSB

Is your house a storehouse of wisdom and knowledge? Hopefully so, because your children and grandchildren need both. Knowledge is found in textbooks. Wisdom, on the other hand, is found in God's Holy Word and in the carefully chosen words of loving parents and thoughtful grandparents.

When we give our children the gift of knowledge, we do them a wonderful service. Knowledge is an important building block in a well-lived life, and it pays rich dividends both personally and professionally. But wisdom is even more important, because it refashions not only the mind but also the heart. And when it comes to sharing the gift of wisdom, savvy grandparents like you have much to offer. So don't hesitate to share the lessons you've learned, because they're lessons that *your* kids, and *their* kids, most certainly need to know.

Let us remember that the longer we live,
the more we know, and the more we know,
the more beautiful we are.
Marianne Williamson

The Importance of Your Smile

A happy heart makes the face cheerful.
Proverbs 15:13 NIV

Okay, Grandmother, it's been a typical day. You've cared for your family, worked hard, perhaps rushed from point A to point Z. But have you taken time to smile? If so, you're a very wise woman. If not, it's time to slow down, take a deep breath, and recount your blessings!

God's joy is always available to us; our challenge is to accept it. And it's up to each of us to claim the Creator's spiritual riches for ourselves.

Would you like to experience the peace that passes mortal understanding? Then accept God's gifts and lay claim to His promises. And put a smile on your face that stretches all the way down to your heart. When you do, you'll discover that when you smile at God, He smiles back.

Every time you smile at someone,
it is an action of love, a gift to that person,
a beautiful thing.
Mother Teresa

Teaching the Rewards of Discipline

Apply your heart to discipline and your ears
to words of knowledge.
Proverbs 23:12 NASB

Wise grandparents (like you) teach their children and grandchildren the importance of discipline, using both words and examples, with a decided emphasis on the latter. After all, life's greatest rewards seldom fall into our laps; to the contrary, our greatest accomplishments usually require lots of work, which is perfectly fine with God. After all, He knows that we're up to the task.

God has big plans for us, plans that He knows we can accomplish if we're willing to work hard and work smart.

The world often conspires to teach our kids that it's perfectly okay to look for shortcuts. But we must teach our families that success is earned by working hard, not by getting by. When we teach our kids and grandkids to work diligently and consistently, they can expect to earn rich rewards for their efforts. But our youngsters must never expect their rewards to precede their labors.

If I could just hang in there, being faithful to my own
tasks, God would make me joyful and content. The
responsibility is mine, but the power is His.
Peg Rankin

Making the Most of Life

He who pursues righteousness and love finds life,
prosperity and honor.
Proverbs 21:21 NIV

Of course, you've heard the saying, "Life is what you make it." And although that statement may seem trite, it's also true. You can choose a life filled to the brim with frustration and fear, or you can choose a life of abundance and peace. That choice is up to you—and only you—and it depends, to a surprising extent, upon your attitude.

What's your attitude today, Grandmother? And what's the prevailing attitude of the people who live under your roof?

God created you (and yours) in His own image, and He wants you (and yours) to experience joy, contentment, peace, and abundance. But God will not force you to experience these things; you must claim them for yourselves. And when is the best time to start reaping the rewards of positive thinking? Right now, of course, if not sooner.

It is God to whom and with whom we travel,
and while He is the End of our journey,
He is also at every stopping place.
Elisabeth Elliot

When Life Is Difficult

*Be strong and courageous. Do not be terrified;
do not be discouraged, for the L*ORD *your God
will be with you wherever you go.*
Joshua 1:9 NIV

This world can be a dangerous and daunting place, so even if you're the most faithful grandmother in town, you may still find your courage tested by the inevitable disappointments and unspoken fears that accompany life here in the new millennium.

The next time you find your courage tested to the limit, remember to take your fears to God. If you call upon Him, you will be comforted. Whatever your challenge, whatever your trouble, God can help you tackle it.

So don't spend too much time fretting over yesterday's failures or tomorrow's dangers. Focus, instead, on today's opportunities . . . and rest assured that God is big enough to meet every challenge you face . . . beginning now and ending never.

*What is courage? It is the ability to be strong in trust, in
conviction, in obedience.
To be courageous is to step out in faith—
to trust and obey, no matter what.*
Kay Arthur

God's Guidance

The steps of the godly are directed by the LORD.
He delights in every detail of their lives.
Psalm 37:23 NLT

God is intensely interested in each of us, and He will guide our steps if we let Him. When we offer heartfelt prayers to Him, and when we strive to follow in the footsteps of His Son, He gives direction and meaning to our lives—but He won't force us to follow Him. To the contrary, God has given us the gift of free will, the ability to understand His instructions and follow them . . . or not.

Will you trust God to guide your steps, Grandmother? You should. When you entrust your life to Him without reservation, God will give you the courage to face any trial, the strength to meet any challenge, and the wisdom to live in His peace. So trust Him today and seek His guidance. When you do, your next step will be the right one.

Are you serious about wanting God's guidance to become
a personal reality in your life? The first step is to tell God
that you know you can't manage your own life; that you
need his help.
Catherine Marshall

When Times Are Stressful

I cried out to the LORD in my suffering, and he heard me.
He set me free from all my fears.
Psalm 34:6 NLT

Every grandparent knows that stressful days are an inevitable fact of modern life. And how do we deal with the challenges of being a busy adult in a demanding, twenty-first-century world? By turning our days and our lives over to God.

Elisabeth Elliot writes, "If my life is surrendered to God, all is well. Let me not grab it back, as though it were in peril in His hand but would be safer in mine!" And her words ring true, especially in these troubled times. When times are tough, when daily stresses threaten to overwhelm us, God remains steadfast, always ready to calm our fears and redirect our steps.

So the next time you feel stressed, Grandmother, call time out and call on God. He's always with you, always loving, always ready to help. And the rest, of course, is up to you.

Don't be overwhelmed.
Take it one day and one prayer at a time.
Stormie Omartian

What the World Needs Now Is Encouragement

*Two are better than one because they have
a good reward for their efforts.
For if either falls, his companion can lift him up. . . .*
Ecclesiastes 4:9–10 HCSB

Do you delight in the victories of others, Grandmother? You should. After all, each day provides countless opportunities to encourage others and to praise their good works. When you do so, you spread seeds of joy and happiness (which, by the way, is a very good thing to do).

You live is a society that has turned criticism into an art form: movie critics, political pundits, talk-show tantrum throwers, angry critics, urbane critics, critics, critics, and more critics. But even if criticism has become a national pastime, the regular folks you encounter on a daily basis need less criticism, not more. In fact, what they really need is encouragement, preferably in large doses.

So today, make sure to put a smile on your face and keep a steady stream of encouraging words on your lips. By honoring others, you will honor your Creator. And everybody wins.

*A really great person is the person who makes
every person feel great.*
G. K. Chesterton

God First

*Honor G*OD *with everything you own;*
give him the first and the best.
Your barns will burst, your wine vats will brim over.
Proverbs 3:9–10 MSG

As you think about the nature of your relationship with God, remember this: you will always have some type of relationship with Him—it is inevitable that your life must be lived in relationship to God. The question is not if you will have a relationship with Him; the burning question is whether or not that relationship will be one that seeks to honor Him . . . or not.

Are you willing to place God first in your life? Unless you can honestly answer this question with a resounding yes, then your relationship with God isn't what it might be, what it could be, or what it should be. Thankfully, God is always available, He's always ready to forgive, and He's waiting to hear from you now. The rest, Grandmother, is up to you.

God deserves first place in your life . . . and you deserve
the experience of putting Him there.
Marie T. Freeman

Be Bold!

God doesn't want us to be shy with his gifts,
but bold and loving and sensible.
2 Timothy 1:7 MSG

How does God intend for us to live? Does He want us to be timid and fearful, or does He intend for us to be confident and bold? The answer should be obvious. God offers us strength and the courage whenever we are wise enough to ask for them. Yet sometimes we may be tempted to take the easy way out even though God may be directing us toward a different, more difficult path.

Today, Grandmother, be bold in the service of your Creator, and encourage your loved ones to do likewise. Face your fears and do your best, knowing that with God on your side, you are protected. When you live courageously, you'll be a marvelous example to your children and grandchildren. But more important, God will bless your efforts and use you in ways that only He can understand.

Let us arm ourselves against our spiritual enemies with
courage. They think twice about engaging
with one who fights boldly.
St. John Climacus

Media Messages and You

To acquire wisdom is to love oneself;
people who cherish understanding will prosper.

Proverbs 19:8 NLT

Sometimes it's hard to have self-respect, especially if you pay much attention to all those messages that media keeps pumping out. Those messages, which seem to pop up just about everywhere, try to tell you how you and your family should look, how you should behave, and what you should buy.

The media isn't interested in making you feel better about yourself—far from it. The media is interested in selling you products. And one of the best ways that marketers can find to sell you things is by making you feel dissatisfied with your current situation. That's why the media works 24/7 to rearrange your priorities.

So, Grandmother, here's a word of warning: don't fall prey to the media's messages, and don't let your grandkids fall prey either. You and your grandchildren are wonderful just as you are . . . don't let anyone tell you otherwise.

The world's sewage threatens to contaminate
the stream of Christian thought.
Is the world shaping your mind, or is Christ?

Billy Graham

He Never Stops Teaching Us

He tells us everything over and over again,
a line at a time, in very simple words!
Isaiah 28:10 NLT

When it comes to learning life's lessons, we can either do things the easy way or the hard way. The easy way can be summed up as follows: when God teaches us a lesson, we learn it . . . the first time! Unfortunately, too many of us—both parents and children alike—learn much more slowly than that.

When we resist God's instruction, He continues to teach, whether we like it or not. And if we keep making the same old mistakes, God responds by rewarding us with the same old results.

Our challenge, then, is to discern God's lessons from the experiences of everyday life. Hopefully, we learn those lessons sooner rather than later, because the sooner we do, the sooner He can move on to the next lesson and the next, and the next . . .

All of life is a constant education.

Eleanor Roosevelt

Beyond Envy

Let us not become boastful, challenging one another, envying one another.

Galatians 5:26 NASB

In a competitive, cutthroat world, it is easy to become envious of others' success. But it's wrong.

We know intuitively that envy is wrong, but because we are frail, imperfect human beings, we may find ourselves struggling with feelings of envy or resentment, or both. These feelings may be especially forceful when we see other people experience unusually good fortune.

Have you recently felt the pangs of envy creeping into your heart? If so, it's time to focus on the marvelous things that God has done for you and your family. And just as important, you must refrain from preoccupying yourself with the blessings that God has chosen to give others.

So here's a surefire formula for a happier, healthier life: count your own blessings, and let your neighbors counts theirs. It's the godly way to live.

Discontent dries up the soul.
Elisabeth Elliot

Enduring Difficult Days

*The LORD is a shelter for the oppressed,
a refuge in times of trouble. Those who know your name
trust in you, for you, O LORD, have never abandoned
anyone who searches for you.*

Psalm 9:9–10 NLT

All of us face difficult days. Sometimes even the most saintly men and women can become discouraged, and you are no exception. Hard times visit every family, so you should prepare yourself and your loved ones for life's inevitable darker days. What's required is a combination of faith, work, wisdom, courage, and teamwork. When your family stands united in the face of adversity, no problem is too big for you to tackle.

If you and your loved ones find yourselves enduring difficult circumstances, remember that here on earth, adversity is the price of admission. But remember this as well: despite life's occasional hardships, when it comes to writing your own stories, the final endings are always up to you.

*In my weakness, I have learned, like Moses, to lean hard
on God. The weaker I am, the harder I lean on Him.
The harder I lean, the stronger I discover Him to be. The
stronger I discover God to be, the more resolute I am in
this job He's given me to do.*

Joni Eareckson Tada

When Things Aren't Perfect

*May Your faithful love comfort me,
as You promised Your servant.*
Psalm 119:76 HCSB

It's an inevitable fact of life: because you are an imperfect human being, you are not perfectly happy—and that's perfectly okay with God. He is far less concerned with your happiness than He is with your holiness.

God continuously reveals Himself in everyday life, but He does not do so in order to make you contented; He does so in order to lead you back to Him. So don't be overly concerned with your current level of happiness: it will change. Be more concerned with the current state of your relationship with the Creator: He does not change. And because your heavenly Father transcends time and space, you can be comforted in the knowledge that in the end His joy will become your joy . . . for all eternity.

*God's goal is not to make you happy.
It is to make you his.*
Max Lucado

April

Thank-You Hug for Grandmother

Dear Grandmother,

    You have always nurtured our family, and we've noticed. Even when we've made mistakes, and even when we've been difficult to live with, you've always been there for us. Leading a family is incredibly hard work, and you have been incredibly faithful. And we are incredibly grateful.

April 1

Beyond All the Regrets

Don't be wishing you were someplace else or with someone else. Where you are right now is God's place for you. Live and obey and love and believe right there.
1 Corinthians 7:17 MSG

Bitterness and regret are emotions that can destroy you if you let them . . . so don't let them!

If you are caught up in intense feelings of anger or regret, you know all too well the destructive power of these emotions. How can you rid yourself of these feelings? First, you must prayerfully ask God to free you from these self-defeating emotions. Then, you must learn to catch yourself whenever thoughts of bitterness begin to attack you. Your challenge is simply this: you must learn to resist negative thoughts before they hijack your emotions, not after.

Christina Rossetti had this sound advice: "Better by far you should forget and smile than you should remember and be sad." And she was right—it's better to forget than regret.

The mire caused by our blunders, errors, and failing can become the quicksand that traps us in regret, or it can become the material we use to make building blocks of righteousness.
Susan Lenzkes

Actions and Beliefs

*If the way you live isn't consistent with
what you believe, then it's wrong.*
Romans 14:23 MSG

Is your life a picture book of your creed? If so, Grandmother, congratulations. After all, in describing our beliefs, our actions are always more important than our words. Yet far too many of us spend more energy talking about our beliefs than living by them—with predictable consequences.

Today and every day, Grandmom, be sure that your actions are guided by God's Word and by the conscience that He has placed in your heart. Don't treat your faith as if it were separate from your everyday life. Weave your beliefs into the very fabric of your day. When you do these things, God will honor your good works, and your good works will honor God.

*We are to leave an impression on all those
we meet that communicates whose we are
and what kingdom we represent.*
Lisa Bevere

Patience and More Patience

God blesses the people who patiently endure testing.
Afterward they will receive the crown of life that
God has promised to those who love him.
James 1:12 NLT

Family life demands patience . . . and lots of it! We live in imperfect homes inhabited by imperfect kids and their imperfect parents. Thank goodness family life doesn't have to be perfect to be wonderful!

Sometimes we inherit troubles from other folks (some of whom live under our roofs, and some who don't). On other occasions, we create trouble for ourselves. In either case, what's required is patience.

So here's a reminder: the next time you find your patience tested to the limit by the limitations of others, remember that nobody who inhabits your world is perfect (including you). And remember that the less you manage to focus on people's imperfections, the better for them and for you.

Patience achieves more than force.
Edmund Burke

Growing Up Day by Day

*The Message bears fruit and gets larger and stronger,
just as it has in you. From the very first day you heard
and recognized the truth of what God is doing,
you've been hungry for more.*

Colossians 1:6 MSG

L ife is a grand and glorious classroom; school is always in session; and the rest is up to us. Every day provides opportunities to learn, to grow, and to share our wisdom with the world.

Sometimes, God sends lessons disguised as problems. Sometimes He wraps His messages inside pain or loss or struggle or exhaustion. But no matter our circumstances, the Father never stops teaching. And if we're wise, we never stop looking for His lessons.

When it comes to your faith, God doesn't intend for you to stand still. He wants you to keep learning and growing every day of your life. No matter how "grown-up" you may be, you still have growing to do. And the more you grow, the more beautiful you become, inside and out.

*Kindness in this world will do much to help others, not
only to come into the light,
but also to grow in grace day by day.*

Fanny Crosby

Life Is Better When
You Don't Burn Out

Thank God for this gift, his gift.
No language can praise it enough!
2 Corinthians 9:15 MSG

Each day, as you awaken from sleep and begin the new day, you are confronted with countless opportunities to serve God, to serve your family, and to serve your community. But sometimes these opportunities masquerade as burdens.

If you're trying to do many things for many people, you may feel overworked, overcommitted, and overwhelmed. But it need not be so.

When your daily to-do list starts spilling over onto second and third pages, that may be God's way of telling you to slow down and start smelling a few more roses.

So here's a prescription for a happier, healthier life: (1) view every day as a glorious opportunity; (2) don't overcommit yourself; (3) help as many folks as you can, but don't burn out; (4) don't ever stop thanking God for His blessings; and (5) don't ever forget numbers 1 through 4.

There are people who want to be everywhere
at once, and they get nowhere.
Carl Sandburg

The World . . . and You

Don't copy the behavior and customs of this world,
but let God transform you into a new person
by changing the way you think.
Romans 12:2 NLT

We live in the world, but we must not worship it. Our duty is to place God first and everything else second. But because we are imperfect human beings with imperfect faith, placing God in His rightful place is often difficult. In fact, at every turn, or so it seems, we are tempted to do otherwise.

The twenty-first-century world is a noisy, distracting place filled with countless opportunities for us and our family members to stray from God's will. The world seems to cry out, "Worship me with your time, your money, your energy, and your thoughts!" But God instructs us to do otherwise: He instructs us to worship Him first and to love our neighbors as we love ourselves; everything else must be secondary.

I have a divided heart, trying to love God
and the world at the same time. God says,
"You can't love me as you should
if you love this world too."
Mary Morrison Suggs

The Art of Cooperation

Work at getting along with each other and with God.
Otherwise you'll never get so much as a glimpse of God.
Hebrews 12:14 MSG

Have you and your family members learned the subtle art of cooperation? If so, you have learned the wisdom of give-and-take, not the foolishness of me-first. Cooperation is the art of compromising on many little things while keeping your eye on one big thing: your family.

But here's a word of warning: if you're like most folks, you're probably a little bit headstrong: you probably want most things done in a fashion resembling the popular song "My Way." But, if you are observant, you will notice that those people who always insist upon "my way or the highway" usually end up with "the highway."

A better strategy for all concerned (including you) is to abandon the search for "my way" and search instead for "our way." The happiest families are those in which everybody learns how to give and take . . . with the emphasis on give.

Alone we can do so little.
Together we can do so much.
Helen Keller

In Times of Uncertainty

I have heard your prayer, I have seen your tears;
surely I will heal you.
2 Kings 20:5 NKJV

Women of every generation have experienced adversity, and this generation is no different. Here in the twenty-first-century, we live in times of uncertainty as the world seems to be changing at an ever-increasing pace. Thankfully, although the world continues to change, God's love remains constant. And He remains ready to comfort you and strengthen you whenever you turn to Him.

When you encounter the inevitable challenges of modern life and caring for your family in a fast-changing world, you should never allow yourself to become discouraged. Instead, turn your concerns over to God. When you do, you'll soon discover that challenges will come and challenges will go, but God stands firm—as your faithful protector—today, tomorrow, and forever.

We can take great comfort that
God never sleeps—so we can.
Dianna Booher

The Self-Fulfilling Prophecy

As for me, I will hope continually,
and will praise You yet more and more.

Psalm 71:14 NASB

The self-fulfilling prophecy is alive, well, and living at your house. If you trust God and have faith for the future, your optimistic beliefs will give you direction and motivation.

As you've probably learned by now, Grandmother, your thoughts have the power to lift you up or to hold you down. When you acquire the habit of hopeful thinking, you will have acquired a powerful tool for improving your life. So if you find yourself falling into the spiritual traps of worry and discouragement, take stock of your thoughts. And while you're at it, make it a point to talk to encouraging friends and family members. Finally, learn to take your worries to God and leave them there. After all, God's Word teaches us that He can overcome every difficulty. And when God makes a promise, He keeps it.

If you keep on saying things are going to be bad,
you have a good chance of becoming a prophet.

Isaac Bashevis Singer

Listening to God

> *The one who is from God listens to God's words.*
> *This is why you don't listen,*
> *because you are not from God.*
> John 8:47 HCSB

Sometimes God speaks loudly and clearly. More often, He speaks in a quiet voice—and if you are wise, you will be listening carefully when He does. To do so, you must carve out quiet moments each day to quiet your soul and sense His directions.

Can you quiet yourself long enough to listen to your conscience? Are you attuned to the subtle instructions of your intuition? Are you willing to pray sincerely and then to wait quietly for God's response? Hopefully so. Usually God refrains from sending His messages on stone tablets or city billboards. More often, He communicates in subtler ways. If you sincerely desire to hear His voice, you must listen carefully, and you must do so in the silent corners of your quiet, willing heart.

> *When we come to Jesus stripped of pretensions, with a*
> *needy spirit, ready to listen,*
> *He meets us at the point of need.*
> Catherine Marshall

Cheerful Generosity

Let each one give as he purposes in his heart,
not grudgingly or of necessity;
for God loves a cheerful giver.
2 Corinthians 9:7 NKJV

Are you a cheerful giver? If you're a woman who's intent upon obeying God's instructions, you will be. After all, God's Word makes it clear: When you give, your heavenly Father looks not only at the quality of your gift but also at the condition of your heart. And if you give generously, joyfully, and without complaint, you'll be blessed.

So today, Grandmom, take God's promises to heart and make this pledge to yourself and your Creator: Vow to be a cheerful, generous, courageous giver. Look for people to help, and then help them. The world needs your help, and you need the spiritual rewards that will be yours when you give faithfully, prayerfully, cheerfully . . . and often.

Here lies the tremendous mystery—that God should
be all-powerful, yet refuse to coerce. He summons us
to cooperation. We are honored in being given the
opportunity to participate in His good deeds. Remember
how He asked for help in performing His miracles: Fill the
water pots, stretch out
your hand, distribute the loaves.
Elisabeth Elliot

April 12

Whom Should You Trust?

The one who understands a matter finds success,
and the one who trusts in the LORD will be happy.
Proverbs 16:20 HCSB

Here's another question for you: where will you place your trust today? Will you trust in the ways of the world, or will you trust in the Word and the will of your Creator?

If you aspire to do great things for God's kingdom, you will trust Him completely.

Trusting God means trusting Him in every aspect of your life. You must trust Him with your relationships. You must trust Him with your finances. You must follow His commandments and pray for His guidance. Then you can wait patiently for God's revelations and for His blessings.

When you trust your heavenly Father without reservation, you can rest assured: in His own fashion and in His own time, God will bless you in ways you never could have imagined. So trust Him, and then prepare yourself for the abundance and joy that will most certainly be yours through Him.

God delights to meet the faith of one who looks up to Him
and says, "Lord, You know that
I cannot do this—but I believe that You can!"
Amy Carmichael

God's Truth

*A person who does not have the Spirit does not accept
the truths that come from the Spirit of God.
That person thinks they are foolish and cannot understand
them, because they can only be judged to be true
by the Spirit. The spiritual person is able to judge
all things, but no one can judge him.*

1 Corinthians 2:14–15 NCV

When God's love touches our hearts and our minds, we are confronted by a powerful force: the awesome, irresistible force of God's truth. In response to that force, we will either follow God's lead by allowing Him to guide our thoughts and deeds, or we will resist God's calling and accept the consequences of our mistaken priorities.

Today, Grandmother, as you fulfill the responsibilities that God has placed before you, ask yourself this question: "Do my thoughts and actions bear witness to the ultimate truth that God has placed in my heart, or am I allowing the pressures of everyday life to overwhelm me?" It's a profound question that only you, as a loving grandparent and a thoughtful woman, can answer for yourself. And it may just be one of the most important questions you ask yourself today or, for that matter, any other day.

Those who walk in truth walk in liberty.

Beth Moore

Praying for Protection

*Your love must be real. Hate what is evil,
and hold on to what is good.*

Romans 12:9 NCV

This world is God's creation, and it contains the wonders of His handiwork and of His love. But it also contains countless opportunities to stray from God's will. Yes, temptations are everywhere, or so it seems, and your family deserves to be protected. So your task, as a caring grandmother, is to do all that you can to shield your clan from the temptations, distractions, and dangers of our troubled world. How can you do this? First, you must teach your children—and their children—well. But that's not all. You should also keep praying for your family, continually asking the Creator to protect your loved ones. When you ask, He will hear, and in His own way He will answer.

*We are in a continual battle with the spiritual
forces of evil, but we will triumph when we yield
to God's leading and call on His powerful
presence in prayer.*

Shirley Dobson

Discovering Wholeness

If your sinful nature controls your mind,
there is death. But if the Holy Spirit controls your mind,
there is life and peace.

Romans 8:6 NLT

Until we open our hearts to God, we are never completely whole. Until we have placed our hearts and our lives firmly in the hands of our loving heavenly Father, we are incomplete. Until we discover the peace that passes all understanding—the peace that God promises can and should be ours—we long for a sense of wholeness that continues to elude us no matter how diligently we search.

It is only through God that we discover lasting peace. We may search far and wide for worldly substitutes, but when we seek peace apart from God, we will find neither peace nor God.

Today, as a gift to yourself and your family, lay claim to the peace that really matters: God's peace. And then share it—today, tomorrow, and every day that you live.

Jesus knows one of the greatest barriers to our faith is often
our unwillingness to be made whole—our unwillingness
to accept responsibility—our unwillingness to live without
excuse for our spiritual smallness and immaturity.

Anne Graham Lotz

Don't Expect Them to Be Perfect

*Those who show mercy to others are happy,
because God will show mercy to them.*

Matthew 5:7 NCV

No one is perfect; neither are one's children. And, of course, no husband is perfect either. But despite their imperfections, every single member of your family is a unique gift from the Creator. And you should treat His gifts with the care and respect they deserve. So refrain from the temptation to lecture or scold. Be slow to anger and quick to forgive. Put an end to negativity; focus, to the best of your abilities, on the positive; and know what to overlook.

The next time a member of your clan makes a mistake, don't criticize or complain. Instead, make it a point to forgive and forget as quickly as possible. Until the day that you become perfect, don't expect others to be.

*Do not think of the faults of others
but of what is good in them
and faulty in yourself.*

St. Teresa of Ávila

Getting Excited About Today

*This is the day which the LORD has made;
let us rejoice and be glad in it.*

Psalm 118:24 NASB

A re you looking forward to the coming day with a mixture of anticipation and excitement? Or are you a little less enthused than that? Hopefully, you're excited about—and thankful for—the coming day.

Nobody (including you) needs to be reminded that some days are filled with sweetness and light, while other days aren't. But even on the darker days of life, you have much to celebrate, including, but not limited to, your life and your loved ones.

As a parent, grandparent, and citizen of the world, you have incredibly important work to do. And you have a vitally important message to share with your family. Share that message with gusto. Your family needs your enthusiasm, and you deserve the rewards that will be yours when you share your wisdom enthusiastically and often.

*A person's mind is not a container to be filled
but rather a fire to be kindled.*

Dorothea Brande

Keeping Things in Perspective

> *All I'm doing right now, friends, is showing how these
> things pertain to Apollos and me so that you will learn
> restraint and not rush into making judgments without
> knowing all the facts. It's important to look at things from
> God's point of view. I would rather not see you inflating or
> deflating reputations based on mere hearsay.*
>
> 1 Corinthians 4:6 MSG

For most of us, life is busy and complicated. Amid
the pressures of the daily grind, it is easy to lose
perspective . . . easy, but wrong. When times are
tough, we can regain perspective by slowing down and
then turning our thoughts and prayers toward God.

So here's a question for you, Grandmother: are
you determined to keep things in perspective, and
have you made up your mind to teach your family
to do likewise? If so, you'll be happy you did, and so
will they.

When you focus your thoughts on your blessings,
not your misfortunes, God will smile on you and
yours. So do yourself and your loved ones a favor:
Learn to think optimistically about the world you live
in and the life you lead. Then prepare yourself for the
blessings that good thoughts will bring.

An optimistic mind is a healthy mind.

Loretta Young

God's Protection

I will lift up my eyes to the hills–from whence comes
my heart? My help comes from the LORD,
who made heaven and earth.
Psalm 121:1–2 NKJV

As a busy woman, you know from firsthand experience that life is not always easy. But as a recipient of God's grace, you also know that you are protected by a loving heavenly Father.

In times of trouble, God will comfort you; in times of sorrow, He will dry your tears. When you are troubled or weak or sorrowful, God is neither distant nor disinterested. To the contrary, God is always present and always vitally engaged in the events of your life. Reach out to Him, and build your future on the Rock that cannot be shaken . . . trust in God and rely upon His provisions. He can provide everything you really need . . . and far, far more.

Through all of the crises of life–
and we all are going to experience them–
we have this magnificent Anchor.
Franklin Graham

April 20

Every Day Should Be Thanksgiving

> *Our prayers for you are always spilling over into thanksgivings. We can't quit thanking God our Father and Jesus our Messiah for you!*
>
> Colossians 1:3 MSG

Sometimes, life here on earth can be complicated, demanding, and busy. When the demands of life leave us rushing from place to place with scarcely a moment to spare, we may fail to pause and say a word of thanks for all the good things we've received. But when we fail to count our blessings, we rob ourselves of the happiness, the peace, and the gratitude that should rightfully be ours as children of God.

Today, even if you're busily engaged in life, slow down long enough to start counting your blessings. You most certainly will not be able to count them all, but take a few moments to jot down as many blessings as you can. Then give thanks to the Giver of all good things: God. His love for you is eternal, as are His gifts. And it's never too soon—or too late—to offer Him thanks.

> *God is in control, and therefore in everything I can give thanks, not because of the situation, but because of the One who directs and rules over it.*
>
> Kay Arthur

The Power of Kindness

> God has chosen you and made you his holy people.
> He loves you. So always do these things:
> Show mercy to others, be kind, humble,
> gentle, and patient.
>
> Colossians 3:12 NCV

Never underestimate the power of kindness. You never know what kind word or gesture will significantly change someone's day or week or life.

Is your home like the Old West, a place "where never is heard a discouraging word and the skies are not cloudy all day" . . . or is the forecast at your house slightly cloudier than that? If your house is a place where the rule of the day is the Golden Rule, don't change a thing. Kindness starts at home, but it should never end there.

So today, slow down and be alert for those who need your smile, your kind words, or your helping hand. Make kindness a centerpiece of your dealings with others. They will be blessed, and so will you.

> *Sometimes one little spark of kindness is*
> *all it takes to reignite the light of hope in a heart that's*
> *blinded by pain.*
>
> Barbara Johnson

April 22

Solving Life's Riddles

The wisdom from above is first pure, then peace-loving,
gentle, compliant, full of mercy and good fruits,
without favoritism and hypocrisy.
James 3:17 HCSB

Life is an exercise in problem solving. Every day, we are presented with a new assortment of questions, decisions, puzzles, and challenges. Thankfully, the riddles of everyday living are not too difficult to solve if we look for answers in the right places. When we have questions, we should consult God's Word, trust the counsel of God-fearing friends and family members, and listen carefully to the conscience God has placed in our hearts.

Are you facing a difficult decision, Grandmother? If so, take your concerns to God, and avail yourself of the messages and mentors He has placed along your path. When you do, God will speak to your conscience in His own way and in His own time, and when He does, you can most certainly trust the answers He gives.

We need to be able to make decisions based on
what we know rather than on what we feel.
Joyce Meyer

April 23

Prayer and Peace

*"Relax, Daniel," he continued, "don't be afraid.
From the moment you decided to humble yourself
to receive understanding, your prayer was heard,
and I set out to come to you."*

Daniel 10:12 MSG

Do you seek a more peaceful life? Then you should
lead a prayerful life. Do you have questions that
you simply can't answer? Ask for the guidance of your
Father in heaven. Do you sincerely seek the gift of
everlasting love and eternal life? Accept the grace of
God's only begotten Son.

When you weave the habit of prayer into the very
fabric of your day, you invite God to become a partner
in every aspect of your life. When you consult God
on a constant basis, you avail yourself of His wisdom,
His strength, and His love. And because God answers
prayers according to His perfect timetable, your
petitions to Him will transform your family, your
world, and yourself. So be good to yourself. Pray
often. It's the peaceful way to live.

*I have been driven many times to my knees
by the overwhelming conviction
that I had absolutely no other place to go.*

Abraham Lincoln

Your Great Expectations

When dreams come true, there is life and joy.
Proverbs 13:12 NLT

Hey Grandmother, do you expect your future to be bright? Are you willing to dream king-sized dreams for yourself and your family . . . and are you willing to work diligently to make those dreams come true? Hopefully so—after all, God promises that we can do "all things" through Him. Yet most of us, even the most devout among us, live far below our potential. We take half measures; we dream small dreams; we waste precious time and energy on the distractions of the world. But God has other plans for us.

Our Creator intends that we live faithfully, hopefully, courageously, and abundantly. He knows that we are capable of so much more, He wants us to do the things we're capable of doing, and He wants us to begin doing those things today.

God created us with an overwhelming desire to soar.
He designed us to be tremendously productive and
"to mount up with wings like eagles," realistically
dreaming of what He can do with our potential.
Carol Kent

Teaching Obedience

*Follow the whole instruction the LORD your God has
commanded you, so that you may live, prosper,
and have a long life in the land you will possess.*

Deuteronomy 5:33 HCSB

As loving grandparents, we must teach our children
and grandchildren to obey the rules of society
and the laws of God. God's laws are contained in a
guidebook for righteous living called the Holy Bible.
It contains thorough instructions, which, if followed,
lead to fulfillment, peace, and righteousness. But,
if we choose to ignore God's commandments, for
whatever reason, the results are as predictable as they
are tragic.

Talking about obedience is easy; living obediently
is considerably harder. But if we are to be responsible
role models for our families and friends, we must
study God's Word and follow it.

So today, Grandmother, as you consider the
lessons that you intend to teach your children (or
your children's children), remember to stress the
importance of obedience. It's a lesson that never goes
out of fashion.

*Obey God one step at a time,
then the next step will come into view.*
Catherine Marshall

Your Passion for Life

*Never be lacking in zeal,
but keep your spiritual fervor, serving the Lord.*
Romans 12:11 NIV

Are you passionate about your life, your work, your family, and your faith? As the recipient of God's blessings, and as the grandmother of your clan, you have every reason to be enthusiastic about life. Of course, sometimes the struggles of everyday living may leave you feeling decidedly unenthusiastic, even discouraged. If you feel that your zest for life is slowly fading away, it's time to slow down, rest, count your blessings, and pray. When you feel worried or weary, you must pray fervently for God to renew your sense of wonderment and excitement.

Life with God is a glorious adventure; revel in it. When you do, God will most certainly smile upon your work, your family, and your life.

*Everything you love is what makes
a life worth living.*
John Eldredge

Watch the Ants

*Go watch the ants, you lazy person. Watch what they do
and be wise. Ants have no commander, no leader or ruler,
but they store up food in the summer and gather their
supplies at harvest. How long will you lie there,
you lazy person? When will you get up from sleeping?*

Proverbs 6:6–9 NCV

The Bible instructs us that we can learn an
important lesson from a surprising source: ants.
Ants are among nature's most industrious creatures.
They do their work without supervision and without
hesitation. We should do likewise.

God's Word is clear: We are instructed to work
diligently and faithfully. We are told that the fields
are ripe for the harvest, that the workers are few,
and that the importance of our work is profound.
Let us labor, then, without hesitation and without
complaint. Nighttime is coming. Until it does, let us
honor our heavenly Father with grateful hearts and
willing hands.

*God provides the ingredients for our daily bread
but expects us to do the baking.
With our own hands!*
Barbara Johnson

Sad Days

*This is what the LORD Almighty says: Once again old men
and women will walk Jerusalem's streets with a cane and
sit together in the city squares. And the streets of the city
will be filled with boys and girls at play.*

Zechariah 8:4–5 NLT

Some days are light and happy, and some days are
not. When we face the inevitable dark days of life,
we must choose how we will respond. Will we allow
ourselves to sink even deeper into our own sadness,
or will we do the difficult work of pulling ourselves
out? We bring light to the dark days of life by turning
first to God and then to trusted family members
and friends. Then we must go to work solving the
problems that confront us. When we do, the clouds
will eventually part, and the sun will shine once more
upon our souls.

So the next time you face one of those sad days
when your emotions are flatter than a watery pancake,
try this: pray for God's strength, share your burdens
with people you trust, and do something constructive.
When you do, you won't stay down for long.

*God is good, and heaven is forever.
These two facts should brighten up
even the darkest day.*

Marie T. Freeman

Surrounded by Opportunities

Make the most of every opportunity.
Colossians 4:5 NIV

As you look at the landscape of your own life and the lives of your loved ones, do you see opportunities, possibilities, and blessings, or do you focus, instead, upon the more negative scenery? If you've acquired the unfortunate habit of focusing too intently upon the negative aspects of life, then your spiritual vision is in need of correction.

Whether you realize it or not, opportunities are whirling around you like stars crossing the night sky: beautiful to observe and too numerous to count. Yet you may be too concerned with the challenges of everyday living to notice those opportunities. That's why you and your loved ones should slow down occasionally, catch your breath, and focus your thoughts on two things: the talents God has given you and the opportunities He has placed before you. God is leading you in the direction of those opportunities. Your task is to watch carefully, pray fervently, and act accordingly.

Life is a glorious opportunity.
Billy Graham

Living Triumphantly and Well

Whoever finds me finds life and receives
favor from the LORD.
Proverbs 8:35 NIV

Are you living the triumphant life that God has promised, or are you, instead, something of a spiritual shrinking violet? As you ponder that question, Grandmother, consider this: God does not intend that you live a life that is commonplace or mediocre. In short, God wants you to live a triumphant life so that others might know precisely what it means to follow Him.

Your life should be akin to a victory celebration, a daily exercise in thanksgiving and praise. So join that celebration today. And while you're at it, make sure that you let everybody know you've joined.

*Every moment and every event of every man's life on earth
plants something in his soul. For just as the wind carries
thousands of winged seeds, so each moment
brings with it germs of spiritual vitality that come to rest
imperceptibly in the minds and wills of men.
Most of these unnumbered seeds perish and are lost,
because men are not prepared to receive them:
for such seeds as these cannot spring up anywhere
except in the good soil of freedom, spontaneity, and love.*
Thomas Merton

May

Thank-You Hug for Grandmother

Dear Grandmother,

Thanks for listening . . . and for trying your best to understand. Sometimes you must have been frustrated by the things we said and did. But you listened anyway. And sometimes you understood us far better than we understood ourselves.

Of course you were willing to share your advice (which, we regret to admit, we sometimes ignored), but you were also willing to let us make our own mistakes without saying, "I told you so."

Even when our words must have seemed silly or repetitive, you kept listening. And that made all the difference.

Gentleness of Spirit

*Your beauty should not come from outward adornment,
such as braided hair and the wearing of gold jewelry and
fine clothes. Instead, it should be that of your inner self,
the unfading beauty of a gentle and quiet spirit,
which is of great worth in God's sight.*

1 Peter 3:3–4 NIV

At times it's difficult to be gentle. As frail human beings, we are subject to the normal frustrations of daily life, and when we are, we are tempted to strike out in anger.

As long as you live here on earth, Grandmother, you will face countless opportunities to lose your temper over small, relatively insignificant events: a traffic jam, a spilled cup of coffee, an inconsiderate comment, a broken promise.

When you are tempted to lose your temper over the inevitable inconveniences of life, don't do it. Turn away from anger and turn instead to your Creator. When you do, you'll discover that God can restore your sense of perspective, and He can fill you with a loving spirit that will help you deal gently and generously with others.

*Nothing is as strong as gentleness,
nothing so gentle as real strength.*

St. Francis de Sales

God Responds

Rejoice evermore. Pray without ceasing.
In every thing give thanks: for this is the will of God
in Christ Jesus concerning you.
1 Thessalonians 5:16–18 KJV

When we petition God, He responds. God's hand is not absent, and it is not distant. It is responsive.

On his second missionary journey, Paul started a small church in Thessalonica. A short time later, he penned a letter that was intended to encourage the new believers at that church. Today, almost two thousand years later, 1 Thessalonians remains a powerful, practical guide for Christian living.

In his letter, Paul advises members of the new church to "pray without ceasing." His advice applies to Christians of every generation, including our own. When we weave the habit of prayer into the very fabric of our days, we invite God to become a partner in every aspect of our lives. When we consult God on an hourly basis, we avail ourselves of His wisdom, His strength, and His love.

Today, allow the responsive hand of God to guide you and help you. Pray without ceasing, and then rest assured: God is listening . . . and responding!

Prayer succeeds when all else fails.
E. M. Bounds

You're Part of His Plan

*Let us not become weary in doing good,
for at the proper time we will reap a harvest
if we do not give up.*
Galatians 6:9 NIV

As you continue to seek God's purpose for your life, you will undoubtedly experience your fair share of disappointments, detours, false starts, and failures. When you do, don't become discouraged: God's not finished with you yet.

The old saying is as true today as it was when it was first spoken: "Life is a marathon, not a sprint." That's why wise travelers (and wise grandmothers!) select a traveling companion who never tires and never falters. That partner, of course, is your heavenly Father.

Today, Grandmother, pray as if everything depended upon God, and work as if everything depended upon you. And while you're at it, have faith that you play an important role in God's great plan for His big, beautiful world—because you do.

*Become so wrapped up in something
that you forget to be afraid.*
Lady Bird Johnson

Saved by Hope

We are saved by hope.
Romans 8:24 KJV

As we all know, hope can be a perishable commodity. Despite God's promises, and despite our countless blessings, we are, at times, frail and fearful human beings, and we can still lose hope from time to time. When we do, we need the encouragement of close friends and family members, and we need the healing touch of God's hand.

Even though this world can be a place of trials and struggles, God has promised us peace, joy, and eternal life if we entrust our lives to Him.

Are you a grandmother who asks God to move mountains in your life, or are you expecting Him to stumble over molehills? So ask for His help today—with faith and with fervor—and then watch in amazement as your mountains begin to move.

Down through the centuries in times of trouble and trial, God has brought courage to the hearts of those who love Him. The Bible is filled with assurances of God's help and comfort in every kind of trouble which might cause fears to arise in the human heart. You can look ahead with promise, hope, and joy.
Billy Graham

When Your Faith Is Tested

*When you are in distress and all these things have
happened to you, you will return to the LORD your God in
later days and obey Him. He will not leave you, destroy
you, or forget the covenant with your fathers
that He swore to them by oath, because the LORD
your God is a compassionate God.*
Deuteronomy 4:30–31 HCSB

When the sun is shining and all is well, it is easy to have faith. But when life takes an unexpected turn for the worse, as it will from time to time, your faith will be tested. In times of trouble and doubt, God remains faithful to you—and you must retain faith in yourself.

Social activist Jane Addams observed, "You do not know what life means when all the difficulties are removed. It's like eating a sweet dessert the first thing in the morning." And so it is with your own life.

So the next time you spot storm clouds on the horizon, remind yourself that every difficult day must come to an end . . . and when times are tough, tough moms and grandmoms (like you) are even tougher.

*God does not help us by removing the tests,
but by making the tests work for us.*
Warren Wiersbe

Living in Our Material World

*Let us lay aside every weight and the sin that so easily
ensnares us, and run with endurance the race
that lies before us, keeping our eyes on Jesus,
the source and perfecter of our faith.*

Hebrews 12:1–2 HCSB

On the grand stage of a well-lived life, material possessions should play a rather small role. Of course, we all need the basic necessities of life, but once we meet those needs for ourselves and for our families, the piling up of possessions creates more problems than it solves. Our real riches, of course, are not of this world. We are never really rich until we are rich in spirit.

Do you sometimes find yourself wrapped up in the concerns of the material world? If so, you're not the only person in your neighborhood to do so. Thankfully, the trap of materialism is a trap you can escape by turning your thoughts and your prayers to more important matters. When you do, you'll begin storing riches that will endure throughout eternity: the spiritual kind.

*When we put people before possessions
in our hearts, we are sowing seeds
of enduring satisfaction.*

Beverly LaHaye

Seeking His Wisdom

Does not wisdom call out? Does not understanding
raise her voice? On the heights along the way,
where the paths meet, she takes her stand.
Proverbs 8:1–2 NIV

Do you seek wisdom for yourself and for your family? Of course you do. But as a thoughtful woman living in a society that is filled with temptations and distractions, you know that it's all too easy for families to stray far from the source of the ultimate wisdom: God's Holy Word.

When you commit yourself to daily study of God's Word—and when you live according to His commandments—you will become wise . . . in time. But don't expect to open your Bible today and be wise tomorrow. Acquiring wisdom takes time.

Today and every day, as a way of understanding God's plan for your life, study His Word and live by it. When you do, you will accumulate a storehouse of wisdom that will enrich your own life and the lives of your family members, your friends, and the world.

Knowledge can be learned, but wisdom must be earned.
Wisdom is knowledge . . . lived.
Sheila Walsh

May 8

Looking for Miracles

*I am the Alpha and the Omega, the Beginning
and the End. I will give to the thirsty from
the spring of living water as a gift.*
Revelation 21:6 HCSB

If you haven't seen any of God's miracles lately, you haven't been looking. Throughout history the Creator has intervened in the course of human events in ways that cannot be explained by science or human rationale. And he's still doing so today.

God's miracles are not limited to special occasions, nor are they witnessed by a select few. God is crafting His wonders all around us: the miracle of the birth of a new baby; the miracle of a world renewing itself with every sunrise; the miracle of lives transformed by God's love and grace. Each day, God's handiwork is evident for all to see and experience.

Today, seize the opportunity to inspect God's hand at work. His miracles come in a variety of shapes and sizes, so keep your eyes and your heart open. Do not become jaded by the pessimism of the world; miracles are real, and they are happening all around us. Be watchful, and you'll soon be amazed.

*Miracles are not contrary to nature but only contrary to
what we know about nature.*
St. Augustine

Celebrating Others

*Let us think about each other and help each other
to show love and do good deeds.*

Hebrews 10:24 NCV

Your loved ones need a regular supply of encouraging words and pats on the back. And you need the rewards that God gives to enthusiastic grandparents who are a continual source of encouragement to their families.

Each day provides countless opportunities to encourage others and to praise their good works. When we do that, we not only spread seeds of joy and happiness, we also follow the commandments of God's Holy Word.

Today, look for the good in others—starting with your family members. And then celebrate the good that you find. When you do, you'll be a powerful force of encouragement in your corner of the world . . . and an enduring blessing to your family.

*The greatest good you can do for another
is not just to share your riches,
but to reveal to him his own.*

Benjamin Disraeli

The Right Way to Solve Problems

People who do what is right may have many problems,
but the Lord will solve them all.

Psalm 34:19 NCV

Face facts, Grandmom, every life is an exercise in problem solving, including yours. The question is not whether you will encounter problems; the real question is how you will choose to address them.

When it comes to solving the problems of everyday living, we often know precisely what needs to be done, but we may be slow in doing it—especially if what needs to be done is difficult or uncomfortable for us. So we put off till tomorrow what should be done today.

The words of Psalm 34 remind us that the Lord solves problems for "people who do what is right." And usually, doing "what is right" means doing the uncomfortable work of confronting our problems sooner rather than later. So with no further ado, let the problem solving begin . . . now.

Often, in the midst of great problems,
we stop short of the real blessing God has for us, which is
a fresh vision of who He is.

Anne Graham Lotz

Complaints?

Do everything without complaining or arguing.
Then you will be innocent and without any wrong.
Philippians 2:14–15 NCV

Because we are imperfect human beings, we sometimes lose sight of our blessings. Ironically, most of us have more blessings than we can count, but we may still find reasons to complain about the minor frustrations of everyday life. To do so, of course, is not only wrong but is a serious roadblock on the path to spiritual growth and abundance.

Our complaints seldom accomplish the positive results we hope to achieve. And to make matters worse, when we complain, we surrender our inner strength and burden those around us.

As a grandparent, you are a vital role model to your grandchildren—and to your grandchildren's parents. So today and every day, make it a practice to count your blessings, not your hardships. It's the truly decent way to live.

Thanksgiving or complaining—these words
express two contrastive attitudes of the souls of God's
children in regard to His dealings with them. The soul
that gives thanks can find comfort
in everything; the soul that complains
can find comfort in nothing.
Hannah Whitall Smith

Your Changing Family

I am the LORD, and I do not change.
Malachi 3:6 NLT

The world is in a state of constant change, and so is your family. Kids are growing up and moving out, loved ones are growing older and passing on, careers begin and end, and the world keeps turning. Everything around you may seem to be in a state of flux, but you can be comforted: although the world is in a state of constant change, God is not.

If your grandchildren seem to be growing up before your eyes, don't panic. And even if other changes in your life are unfolding at a furious pace, your heavenly Father is the Rock that cannot be shaken—He does not change. So rest assured: it is precisely because your heavenly Father does not change that you and your family can face the transitions of life with courage for today and hope for tomorrow.

*Becoming a grandmother is above all
a learning experience.*
Sheila Kitzinger

When Mistakes Become Lessons

The one who conceals his sins will not prosper,
but whoever confesses and renounces them will find mercy.
Proverbs 28:13 HCSB

We are imperfect people living in an imperfect world; mistakes are simply part of the price we pay for being here. But even though mistakes are an inevitable part of life's journey, repeated mistakes should not be. When we commit the inevitable blunders of life, we must correct them, learn from them, and pray to God for the wisdom not to repeat them. And then, if we are successful, our mistakes become lessons, and our lives become adventures in growth, not stagnation.

So, Grandmother, the next time you experience one of life's inevitable setbacks, it's time to start looking for the lesson that God is trying to teach you. It's time to learn what needs to be learned, change what needs to be changed, and move on.

We ought not to look back unless it is to derive useful
lessons from past errors and for the purpose of profiting by
dearly bought experience.
George Washington

His Surprising Plans

*As it is written in the Scriptures: "No one has ever seen
this, and no one has ever heard about it. No one has ever
imagined what God has prepared for those who love him."*
1 Corinthians 2:9 NCV

God has big plans for your family, wonderful,
surprising plans . . . but He won't force those
plans upon you and yours. To the contrary, He has
given you and your family members free will, the
ability to make decisions on your own. Now it's up to
you to make those decisions wisely.

If you and yours seek to live in accordance with
God's plan for your lives, you will associate with people
who, by their words and actions, will encourage your
spiritual growth. You will assiduously avoid those two
terrible temptations: the temptation to disobey the
Creator and the temptation to squander the time He
has given you. And finally, you will listen carefully,
even reverently, to the conscience that the Creator
has placed in your heart.

God intends to use you, Grandmother, in
wonderful, unexpected ways if you let Him. Let Him.
When you do, you'll be thoroughly surprised by the
creativity and the beauty of His plans.

*God will never lead you
where His strength cannot keep you.*
Barbara Johnson

Above and Beyond Guilt

*If we claim that we're free of sin, we're only fooling
ourselves. A claim like that is errant nonsense. On the
other hand, if we admit our sins—make a clean breast of
them—he won't let us down; he'll be true to himself.
He'll forgive our sins and purge us of all wrongdoing.*

1 John 1:8–9 MSG

All of us have made mistakes. Sometimes our
failures result from our own shortsightedness.
On other occasions, we are swept up in events that
are beyond our abilities to control. Under either set
of circumstances, we may experience intense feelings
of guilt. But God has an answer for the guilt we feel.
That answer, of course, is His forgiveness.

When we ask our heavenly Father for His
forgiveness, He forgives us completely and without
reservation. Then we must do the difficult work of
forgiving ourselves in the same way that God has
forgiven us: thoroughly and unconditionally.

So if you're feeling guilty, it's time for a special
kind of housecleaning—a housecleaning of your mind
and your heart . . . beginning now!

*Don't be bound by your guilt or your fears any longer, but
realize that sin's penalty has already
been paid by Christ completely and fully.*

Billy Graham

The Importance of Words

From a wise mind comes wise speech;
the words of the wise are persuasive.
Proverbs 16:23 NLT

How important are the words we speak? More important than we may realize. Our words have echoes that extend beyond place or time. If our words are encouraging, we can lift others up; if our words are hurtful, we can hold others back.

So here's a pair of questions for you and your family to consider: Do you really try to be a source of encouragement to the people you encounter every day? And are you careful to speak words that lift those people up? If so, you will avoid angry outbursts. You will refrain from impulsive outpourings. You will terminate tantrums. Instead, you will speak words of encouragement and hope to friends, to family members, to coworkers, and even to strangers. And by the way, all the aforementioned people have at least one thing in common: they, like just about everybody else in the world, need all the hope and encouragement they can get.

Attitude and the spirit in which we
communicate are as important
as the words we say.
Charles Stanley

The Cornerstone

The LORD is the strength of my life.
Psalm 27:1 KJV

Have you made God the cornerstone of your life, or is He relegated to a few hours on Sunday morning? Have you genuinely allowed God to reign over every corner of your heart—and your house—or have you attempted to place Him in a spiritual compartment? The answer to these questions will determine the direction of your day, not to mention the direction of your life.

God loves you, Grandmother, and He loves every member of your family. He never leaves your side, not even for a moment. He watches over you every moment, and He hears your every prayer.

God stands at the door of your heart and waits. Welcome Him in. And then accept the peace and the strength and the protection and the abundance that only God can give.

God will never lead you where
His strength cannot keep you.
Barbara Johnson

Don't Settle for Second Best

This hope we have as an anchor of the soul,
both sure and steadfast, and which enters
the Presence behind the veil.

Hebrews 6:19 NKJV

Grandmother, do you believe that you deserve the best and that you will receive the best life has to offer? And do you believe your loved ones deserve the best too? Hopefully so.

As you plan for the next stage of your life's journey, promise yourself that when it comes to the important things in life, you won't settle for second best. And what, pray tell, are the "important things"? Your faith, your family, your health, and your relationships, for starters. In each of these areas, you deserve to be a rip-roaring, top-drawer success.

Become sold on yourself—sold on your opportunities, sold on your potential, sold on your abilities, sold on your family. Because if you're sold, chances are the world will soon become sold too, and the results will be beautiful.

The things we think are the things that feed
our souls. If we think on pure and lovely things,
we shall grow pure and lovely like them;
and the converse is equally true.

Hannah Whitall Smith

Infinite Possibilities

I have fought a good fight, I have finished my course,
I have kept the faith.
2 Timothy 4:7 KJV

We live in a world of infinite possibilities. But sometimes, because of limited faith and limited understanding, we wrongly assume that God cannot or will not intervene in our own lives. Such assumptions are simply wrong.

Are you afraid to ask God to do big things in your own life or in the lives of your loved ones? If so, it's time to abandon your doubts, dust off your hopes, and reclaim your faith—faith in yourself, faith in your family, faith in your abilities, faith in your future, and faith in your heavenly Father.

Remember, Grandmother, that no job is too big for God. And make no mistake: God can help you do things you never dreamed possible . . . your job is to let Him.

God's faithfulness and grace make
the impossible possible.
Sheila Walsh

Priorities That Are Pleasing to God

I will instruct you and teach you in the way you should go;
I will counsel you and watch over you.
Psalm 32:8 NIV

Each waking moment holds the potential for you to think a creative thought or offer a heartfelt prayer. And when you sincerely seek to discover God's priorities for your life, He will provide answers in marvelous and surprising ways.

Remember, this is the day God has made, and He has filled it with countless opportunities to love, to serve, and to seek His guidance. Seize those opportunities. And as a gift to yourself, your family, and the world, slow down and establish clear priorities that are pleasing to the Creator. When you do, you will earn the inner peace that is your spiritual birthright, a peace that is yours for the asking. So ask . . . and be thankful.

Every day we live is a priceless gift of God,
loaded with possibilities to learn something new,
to gain fresh insights.
Dale Evans Rogers

Every Day a Celebration

The heavens declare the glory of God,
and the sky proclaims the work of His hands.
Psalm 19:1 HCSB

The Bible teaches us that every day is a custom-made gift from God. How will you receive that gift? Will you celebrate your family and your life? Will you rejoice at God's marvelous creation? And will you do your best to share your joy with others? Hopefully so . . . but if you're hit by the inevitable distractions of everyday living, you may be tempted to put off your celebration till tomorrow. Don't do it! The dawning of every new day, including this one, is a cause to rejoice. And the best moment to accept God's gifts is the present one.

So here are the big questions, Grandmom: will you accept God's blessings now or later? Are you willing to give Him your full attention today? Hopefully so. He deserves it. And so, for that matter, do you.

Don't miss the beautiful colors of the rainbow
while you're looking for the pot of gold
at the end of it!
Barbara Johnson

His Healing Touch

*"I will give peace, real peace, to those far and near,
and I will heal them," says the Lord.*
Isaiah 57:19 NCV

Savvy grandmoms like you are concerned with spiritual, physical, and emotional health. And there's a timeless source of comfort and assurance, an eternal resource for you and your loved ones, that is as near as your next breath. That source of insight and comfort is, of course, God.

God is concerned about every aspect of your life, including your health. And when you face concerns of any sort—including health-related challenges—God is with you.

So trust your medical doctor to do his or her part, and turn to your family and friends for moral, physical, and spiritual support. But don't stop there. For the ultimate source of strength, protection, and wisdom, place your trust in your benevolent heavenly Father. His healing touch, like His love, endures forever.

If you want to receive emotional healing from God and come into an area of wholeness, you must realize that healing is a process, and you must allow the Lord to deal with you and your problem in His own way and in His own time.
Joyce Meyer

Don't Worry About Tomorrow

Seek first his kingdom and his righteousness, and all these things will be given to you as well. Therefore do not worry about tomorrow, for tomorrow will worry about itself. Each day has enough trouble of its own.

Matthew 6:33–34 NIV

If you are like most grandparents, you may on occasion find yourself worrying about health, finances, safety, relationships, family, and countless other challenges of life, some great and some small. Where is the best place to take your worries? Take them to God. And after you've talked to God, it also helps to talk openly to the people who love you, the trusted friends and family members who know you best. The more you talk and the more you pray, the better you'll feel.

Once you've talked things over with friends, family, and God, it's time to get busy fixing what's broken. So instead of worrying about tomorrow, do today's work and leave the rest up to God. When you do, you'll discover that if you do your part today, the future has a way of taking care of itself.

Remember always that there are two things which are more utterly incompatible even than oil and water, and these two are trust and worry.

Hannah Whitall Smith

He Wants Your Attention

Whoever becomes simple and elemental again,
like this child, will rank high in God's kingdom.
Matthew 18:4 MSG

You and your family inhabit a highly complicated society, a place where people and corporations vie for your attention, for your time, for your dollars, and for your life. Don't let them succeed in complicating your world! Instead, keep your eyes focused upon God and upon His will for you and yours.

If your material possessions are somehow distancing you from God, discard them. If your outside interests leave you too little time for your family or your Creator, slow down the merry-go-round or, better yet, get off the merry-go-round completely. And while you're at it, encourage your family to abandon the merry-go-round too.

Today, remember that God wants your full attention, and He wants it now. So don't let anybody or anything divert your attention from Him.

Give God what's right—not what's left!
Author Unknown

The Attitude of Gratitude

Everything created by God is good, and nothing is to be rejected if it is received with gratitude; for it is sanctified by means of the word of God and prayer.

1 Timothy 4:4–5 NASB

For most modern grandparents, life is busy and complicated, but nobody really needs to tell you that. From years of experience, you already know that leading and caring for a family can be a full-time job (thankfully, it's also a very rewarding job indeed).

Sometimes amid the rush and crush of the daily grind, you may find it easy to lose sight of God and His blessings. But when you forget to slow down and say "Thank You" to your Maker, you're unintentionally robbing yourself of His presence, His peace, and His joy.

So, Grandmother, take time to praise the Creator many times each day. Then, with gratitude in your heart, you can face the day's duties with the perspective and power that only He can provide.

No duty is more urgent than that of returning thanks.

St. Ambrose

The Glorious Gift of Life

*Live full lives, full in the fullness of God. God can do
anything, you know—far more than you could ever imagine
or guess or request in your wildest dreams! He does it not
by pushing us around but by working within us,
his Spirit deeply and gently within us.*

Ephesians 3:19–20 MSG

This day, like every other, is filled to the brim with
opportunities, challenges, and choices. But no
choice that you make is more important than the
choice you make concerning God. Today, you will
either place Him at the center of your life—or not—and
the consequences of that choice have implications
that are both temporal and eternal.

Sometimes, without our even realizing it, we
gradually drift away from the One we need most.
Thankfully, God never drifts away from us. He
remains always present, always steadfast, always
loving.

As you begin this day, Grandmother, be sure to
place God where He belongs: in your head, in your
prayers, on your lips, and in your heart. And then,
with the Creator of the universe as your guide and
companion, let the journey begin . . .

*You have a glorious future in Christ!
Live every moment in His power and love.*

Vonette Bright

Depending upon God

*It will come about that whoever calls on the name
of the LORD will be delivered.*

Joel 2:32 NASB

God is a never-ending source of strength and courage if we call upon Him. When we are weary, He gives us strength. When we see no hope, God reminds us of His promises. When we grieve, God wipes away our tears.

Do you feel overwhelmed by the responsibilities of today? Are you mired in yesterday's regrets? Or do you feel pressured by the uncertainty of tomorrow? If so, then turn your concerns and your prayers over to God. He knows your needs, and He has promised to meet those needs. Whatever your circumstances, God will protect you and care for you . . . if you let Him. Invite Him into your heart and allow Him to renew your spirit. When you trust Him completely and without reservation, He will never fail you.

*Worry does not empty tomorrow of its sorrow;
it empties today of its strength.*

Corrie ten Boom

He Is with You Always

I am not alone, because the Father is with Me.
John 16:32 HCSB

Where is God? God is eternally with us. He is omnipresent. He is, quite literally, everywhere you have ever been and everywhere you will ever go. He is with you night and day; He knows your every thought; He hears your every heartbeat.

Sometimes, in the crush of your maternal duties, God may seem far away. Or sometimes, Grandmother, when the disappointments and sorrows of life leave you brokenhearted, God may seem distant to you, but He is not. When you earnestly seek God, you will find Him because He is here, waiting patiently for you to reach out to Him . . . right here . . . right now.

Even though, at first, God's ways might seem harsh to our
human mind, it's only because we cannot comprehend
the glory that God wants to weave into our lives
once the hard shell of our soul has been shattered.
Only then will we know the healing,
the strengthening, the empowering, the rest,
the peace and joy that comes from God's presence.
Nancy Missler

Learning to Live in the Future Tense

Wisdom is pleasing to you.
If you find it, you have hope for the future.
Proverbs 24:14 NCV

Can you find the courage to accept the past by forgiving all those who have injured you (including yourself)? If you can, you can then look to the future with a sense of optimism and hope.

God has instructed you to place our hopes in Him, and He has promised that you will be His throughout eternity. Your task, as a positive role model for—and a concerned leader of—your family, is to take God at His word.

Of course, we all face occasional disappointments and failures while we are here on earth, but these are only temporary defeats. Of course, this world can be a place of trials and tribulations, but we are secure. God has promised us peace, joy, and eternal life. And God keeps His promises today, tomorrow, and forever.

For what has been—thanks!
For what shall be—yes!
Dag Hammarskjöld

Strength for Today

Those who hope in the LORD will renew their strength.
They will soar on wings like eagles; they will run
and not grow weary, they will walk and not be faint.
Isaiah 40:31 NIV

Where do you go to find strength? The gym? The health-food store? The espresso bar? The chocolate shop? These places are all fine, but there's a better source of strength, of course, and that source is God. He can be a never-ending source of power and courage if you call upon Him.

Are you an energized grandmom? Have you tapped in to God's strength? Have you turned your life and your heart over to Him, or are you still muddling along under your own power? The answer to these questions will determine the quality of your day and your life. So start tapping in—and remember that when it comes to strength, God is the Ultimate Source.

As we join together in prayer, we draw on
God's enabling might in a way that multiplies
our own efforts many times over.
Shirley Dobson

Your Future in His Hands

> *I know the thoughts that I think toward you,*
> *says the LORD, thoughts of peace and not of evil,*
> *to give you a future and a hope. Then you will call upon*
> *Me and go and pray to Me, and I will listen to you.*
> Jeremiah 29:11–12 NKJV

Grandmother, here are a few questions worth pondering: Are you willing to place your future in the hands of a loving and all-knowing God? Do you trust in the ultimate goodness of His plan for your life? And will you face today's challenges with optimism and hope? If you answered each of these questions with a resounding yes, congratulations are in order. After all, God created you for a very important reason: His reason. And you have important work to do: His work.

So today, as you live in the present and look to the future, remember that God has a very important plan for you. And while you still have time, it's up to you to act—and to believe—accordingly.

> *Do not limit the limitless God!*
> *With Him, face the future unafraid*
> *because you are never alone.*
> Mrs. Charles E. Cowman

June

Thank-You Hug for Grandmother

Dear Grandmother,

   Thanks for listening to our dreams—and thanks for believing in them. When we summoned the courage to confide in you, you supported us, you encouraged us, and you trusted us. If you harbored any doubts, you hid them.

   Please know that your faith was contagious—and it worked.

Good Pressure, Bad Pressure

Don't envy evil men or desire to be with them.
Proverbs 24:1 HCSB

Our world is filled with pressures: some good, some bad. The pressures to follow God's will and to obey His commandments are positive pressures. God places them on our hearts, and He intends that we act in accordance with these feelings. But we also face different pressures, ones that are definitely not from God. When we feel pressured to do things—or even to think thoughts—that lead us away from God, we must beware.

Are you worried that your grandkids will be tempted to follow the crowd, not God? If so, you're not alone. Parents and grandparents the world over have concerns for their kids, and rightfully so.

As a concerned grandparent, you must do your best to lead your clan by your example and by your words. And you must pray for every member of your family. Then, when you've done these things, leave the rest up to God.

Those who follow the crowd usually get lost in it.
Rick Warren

Specific Prayers

God answered their prayers because they trusted him.
1 Chronicles 5:20 MSG

As the old saying goes, if it's big enough to worry about, it's big enough to pray about. Yet sometimes we don't pray about the specific details of our lives. Instead, we may offer general prayers that are decidedly heavy on platitudes and decidedly light on particulars.

The next time you pray, try this: be very specific about the things you ask God to do. Of course God already knows precisely what you need—He knows infinitely more about your life than you do—but you need the experience of talking to your Creator in honest, unambiguous language.

So today don't be vague with God. Tell Him exactly what you need. He doesn't need to hear the details, but you do.

There will be no power in our lives
apart from prayer.
Angela Thomas

Sharing Your Burdens with God

They cried out to the LORD in their trouble;
He saved them from their distress.
Psalm 107:13 HCSB

The Bible promises this: tough times are temporary but God's love is not—God's love endures forever. So what does that mean to you? Just this: from time to time, everybody faces hardships and disappointments, and so will you. And when tough times arrive, God always stands ready to protect you and heal you. Your task is straightforward: you must share your burdens with Him.

Whatever the size of your challenges, God is big enough to handle them. Ask for His help today, with faith and with fervor. Instead of turning things over in your mind, turn them over to God in prayer. Instead of worrying about your next decision, ask God to lead the way. Cast your burdens upon the One who cannot be shaken, and rest assured that He always hears a grandmother's prayers.

We are not called to be burden-bearers,
but cross-bearers and light-bearers.
We must cast our burdens on the Lord.
Corrie ten Boom

How Do You Define Success?

*If you do not stand firm in your faith,
then you will not stand at all.*
Isaiah 7:9 HCSB

Grandmother, how do you define success? Do you define it as the accumulation of material possessions or the adulation of your neighbors? If so, you need to rethink your priorities. Genuine success has little to do with fame or fortune; it has everything to do with God's gift of love and His promise of spiritual abundance.

Today, take a few minutes to consider your own definition of success. Have you been taken in by the world's definition of "successful living," or have you come to understand that genuine success is defined not by man, but by God? After you've answered that question, and after you've made certain that your priorities are in order, get out there and have a *really* successful day.

*People judge us by the success of our efforts.
God looks at the efforts themselves.*
Charlotte Brontë

The Opportunity to Serve

The one who blesses others is abundantly blessed;
those who help others are helped.
Proverbs 11:25 MSG

Here's a question for you, Grandmother: will you consider each day another opportunity to celebrate life and improve your little corner of the world? Hopefully so, because your corner of the world, like so many other corners of the world, can use all the help it can get.

You can make a difference, a big difference, in the quality of your own life and the lives of your family, your neighbors, your friends, and your community. You make the world a better place whenever you find a need and fill it. And in these difficult days, the needs are great—but so are your abilities to meet those needs.

So as you plan for the day ahead, be sure to make time for service. Father's orders. And then expect good things to happen, as God richly rewards your generosity.

There is nothing small in the service of God.
St. Francis de Sales

Protected by the Creator of the Universe

*The LORD is my rock, my fortress and my deliverer;
the God of my strength, in Him I will trust.*

2 Samuel 22:2–3 NKJV

Have you ever faced challenges that seemed too big to handle? Have you ever faced big problems that, despite your best efforts, simply could not be solved? If so, you know how uncomfortable it is to feel helpless in the face of difficult circumstances. Thankfully, even when there's nowhere else to turn, you can turn your thoughts and prayers to God, and He will respond.

God protects those who turn their hearts and prayers to Him. Count yourself among that number. When you do, you can live courageously and joyfully, knowing that "this too will pass"—but that God's love for you will not. And then, Grandmother, you can draw strength from the knowledge that you are a marvelous creation, loved, protected, and uplifted by the ever-present hand of God.

*He is within and without. His Spirit dwells
within me. His armor protects me.
He goes before me and is behind me.*

Mary Morrison Suggs

When You Look in the Mirror

*A devout life does bring wealth,
but it's the rich simplicity of being yourself before God.*
1 Timothy 6:6 MSG

Here's a simple question for you, Grandmother, and please answer as honestly as you can: are you your own worst critic? If so, it's time to become a little more understanding of the woman whose image appears on your driver's license.

Millions of words have been written about various ways to improve self-image and increase self-esteem. Yet maintaining a healthy self-image is, to a surprising extent, a matter of doing three things: (1) behaving oneself; (2) thinking healthy thoughts; (3) finding meaning in the fabric of everyday life.

The Bible affirms the importance of self-acceptance by teaching Christians to love others as they love themselves (Matthew 22:37–40). God accepts us just as we are. And if He accepts us—faults and all—then who are we to believe otherwise.

*Nobody can make you feel inferior
without your consent.*
Eleanor Roosevelt

Catch the Enthusiasm

A word spoken at the right time is like
golden apples on a silver tray.
Proverbs 25:11 HCSB

Enthusiasm, like other human emotions, is contagious. If you associate with hope-filled, enthusiastic people, their enthusiasm will have a tendency to lift your spirits. But if you find yourself spending too much time in the company of naysayers, pessimists, or cynics, your thoughts, like theirs, will tend to be negative.

So, Grandmother, as you consider ways to improve your spiritual and emotional health, ask yourself if you're associating with positive people. If so, then you can rest assured you're availing yourself of a priceless gift: encouragement.

Today, look for reasons to celebrate God's countless blessings. And while you're at it, look for upbeat friends who will join with you in the celebration. You'll be better for their company, and they'll be better for yours.

Encouragement is to a friendship
what confetti is to a party.
Nicole Johnson

Words Are Never Enough

God's Way is not a matter of mere talk;
it's an empowered life.
1 Corinthians 4:20 MSG

It would be very easy to teach our grandkids everything they need to know about life if we could teach them with words alone. But we can't. Our kids hear some of the things we say, but they watch everything we do.

As parents, we serve as unforgettable role models for our children and our grandchildren. The lives we lead and the choices we make should serve as enduring examples of the rewards that accrue to all who worship God and obey His commandments.

Is your faith demonstrated by the example you set for your children? If so, you will be blessed, and so, in turn, will they. So today, as you fulfill your responsibilities, remember that your family is watching . . . and so, for that matter, is God.

I'd rather see a sermon than hear one any day;
I'd rather one should walk with me
than merely tell the way.
Edgar A. Guest

Claiming Contentment in a Discontented World

*Satisfy us in the morning with your unfailing love,
that we may sing for joy and be glad all our days.*

Psalm 90:14 NIV

Everywhere we turn, or so it seems, the world promises us contentment and happiness. We are bombarded by messages offering us the good life if only we will purchase products and services that claim to provide happiness, success, and contentment. But the contentment the world offers is fleeting and incomplete. Thankfully, the contentment God offers is all-encompassing and everlasting.

Happiness depends less upon our circumstances than upon our thoughts. When we turn our thoughts to God, to His gifts, and to His glorious creation, we experience the joy that God intends for His children. But when we focus on the negative aspects of life, we cause ourselves needless suffering.

So here's a strategy for happiness that's proven and true: claim the spiritual abundance that God offers His children . . . and keep claiming it, Grandmother, day by glorious day, for as long as you live.

*True contentment is the power of getting
out of any situation all that is in it.*

G. K. Chesterton

Healthy Habits

*Beloved, I pray that in all respects you may prosper
and be in good health, just as your soul prospers.*

3 John 1:2 NASB

All habits begin as small, consistent decisions that may seem harmless and insignificant at first. But before long, habits gain the power to change, transform, and even define you. And as the grandmother (and leader) of your family, you're not just forming habits for yourself; you're also helping to shape the habits of your grandkids. So it's always good to take an honest look at the habits that make up the fabric of your day.

Are you and your family members eating and exercising sensibly? Have you established healthy habits that will improve the chances that you and your loved ones will live long, healthy lives? Hopefully so.

Once you establish healthy habits, and when you reinforce those habits every day, you'll be surprised at how quickly your physical, mental, and spiritual health will begin to improve. So why not start forming those healthier habits today?

Begin to be now what you will be hereafter.

St. Jerome

Transformation

His message was simple and austere,
like his desert surroundings:
"Change your life. God's kingdom is here."
Matthew 3:2 MSG

God has the power to transform your life and the lives of your loved ones. And as a thoughtful woman, a caring mother, and a devoted grandmother, it's your job to ask Him to do it.

God stands at the door and waits; all you and your family members must do is knock. When you do, God always answers.

So today and every day, be sure to take every step of your journey with God as your traveling companion. Study His Word, follow His instructions, talk to Him often, and honor His Son. And while you're at it, be an example of the genuine difference that God can make in the lives of people (like you) who trust Him completely. When you do, you'll be transformed, and you'll be blessed . . . now and forever.

God's work is not in buildings,
but in transformed lives.
Ruth Bell Graham

Faith and Wholeness

The just shall live by faith.
Hebrews 10:38 NKJV

In the ninth chapter of Matthew, we are told of a suffering woman who sought healing in a dramatic way: she simply touched the hem of Jesus' garment. When she did, Christ turned and said, "Daughter, be of good comfort; thy faith hath made thee whole" (Matthew 9:22 KJV). We, too, can be made whole when we place our faith completely and unwaveringly in God.

As you learn to trust God more and more, you'll be amazed at the marvelous things He can do with you and through you. So strengthen your faith through praise, through worship, through Bible study, and through prayer. Then, trust God's plans. Your Heavenly Father is standing at the door of your heart. If you reach out to Him in faith, He will give you peace and heal your broken spirit. Be content to touch even the smallest fragment of the Master's garment, and He will make you whole.

God loves us the way we are,
but He loves us too much to leave us that way.
Leighton Ford

Time to Celebrate

Weeping may endure for a night,
but joy comes in the morning.

Psalm 30:5 NKJV

Are you living a life of agitation or celebration? If you're a thoughtful grandmother, it should most certainly be the latter. When you consider the joys and fulfillment that you derive from your family, and when you stop to think about the countless blessings that God has bestowed upon you and yours, you have many reasons to rejoice.

Today, celebrate the life that God has given you. Today, put a smile on your face, kind words on your lips, and a song in your heart. Be generous with your praise and free with your encouragement. And then, when you have celebrated life to the full, invite your friends to do likewise. After all, this is God's day, and He has given us clear instructions for its use. We are commanded to rejoice and be glad. So, with no further ado, let the celebration begin . . .

A joyful heart is like a sunshine of God's love,
the hope of eternal happiness, a burning flame
of God. And if we pray, we will become that sunshine of
God's love—in our own home,
the place where we live, and in the world at large.

Mother Teresa

His Comforting Hand

God, who comforts the downcast, comforted us.
2 Corinthians 7:6 NIV

God is the great Comforter, Grandmother, and He stands ready to comfort you and yours. But sometimes you may not feel like being comforted. At times you may find yourself discouraged by the inevitable disappointments and tragedies that occur in the lives of believers and nonbelievers alike.

The next time you find your faith tested by tough times, lean upon God's promises. Trust His Son. Remember that God is always near and that He is your protector and your deliverer. When you are anxious or afraid, call upon Him and accept the touch of His comforting hand. Remember that God rules both mountaintops and valleys—with limitless wisdom and love—now and forever.

Put your hand into the hand of God.
He gives the calmness and serenity
of heart and soul.
Mrs. Charles E. Cowman

The Power of Perseverance

> *As for you, be strong and do not give up,*
> *for your work will be rewarded.*
> 2 Chronicles 15:7 NIV

Ask almost any successful grandmother about the ups and downs of family life, and she will tell you that the occasional disappointments and failures of life are inevitable. Those occasional setbacks, false starts, and roadblocks are simply the price we all must pay for our willingness to take risks as we follow our dreams. But even when we come face-to-face with failure, we must never lose faith.

Are you willing to keep fighting the good fight, even when you've experienced unexpected difficulties? And are you willing to encourage your children and grandchildren to do the same? If so, you and yours may soon be surprised at the creative ways that God finds to help determined people . . . people (like you) who possess the wisdom and the courage to persevere.

> *You may have to fight a battle*
> *more than once to win it.*
> Margaret Thatcher

He Renews Us

*I will give you a new heart and
put a new spirit within you.*
Ezekiel 36:26 HCSB

God intends for us to lead joyous lives filled with
abundance and peace. But sometimes, as all
women can attest, abundance and peace seem very
far away. It is then that we must turn to God for
renewal, and when we do, He will restore us.

Have you tapped in to the power of God, or are
you muddling along under your own power? If you
are weary, worried, fretful, or fearful, then it is time
to turn to a strength much greater than your own.

The Bible promises that with God all things are
possible. Are you ready to turn things over to Him? If
you do, you'll soon discover that the Creator of the
universe stands ready and able to create a new sense
of wonderment and joy in you.

*Sometimes, we need
a housecleaning of the heart.*
Catherine Marshall

Being Patient with Yourself

You're blessed when you're content with just who you are—
no more, no less. That's the moment you find yourselves
proud owners of everything that can't be bought.
Matthew 5:5 MSG

Being patient with other people can be difficult. But sometimes, we find it even more difficult to be patient with ourselves. We have high expectations of ourselves, and we have lofty goals. We want to accomplish things now, not later. We want to be as perfect as possible, and, of course, we want our lives to unfold according to our own timetables, not God's. But things don't always turn out as planned. Our lives are not perfect, and neither are we.

So, here's a helpful hint, Grandmom, for dealing (happily) with your world and yourself: be patient with all people, beginning with that particular woman who stares back at you each time you gaze into the mirror. That woman is wonderful . . . and she deserves your respect.

When we begin to take our failures non-seriously,
it means we are ceasing to be afraid of them.
It is immensely important to learn
to laugh at ourselves.
Katherine Mansfield

Faith and Family

*The fundamental fact of existence is that
this trust in God, this faith, is the firm foundation
under everything that makes life worth living.*
Hebrews 11:1 MSG

Would you like to strengthen the ties that bind your family together? Here's a wonderful place to start: by strengthening your faith in God.

Every life and every family is a series of successes and failures, celebrations and disappointments, joys and sorrows. Every step of the way, through every triumph and tragedy, God will stand by family and strengthen you. Your job is to let Him do precisely that.

When you and your loved ones place your faith, your trust, indeed your lives in the hands of the Creator, you'll be amazed at the marvelous things He can do with you and through you. So strengthen your faith and your family through praise, through worship, through Bible study, and through prayer. And trust God's plans. He will never let you down.

*Faith is not a feeling; it is action.
It is a willed choice.*
Elisabeth Elliot

His Answer to Our Guilt

If my people who are called by my name will humble themselves and pray and seek my face and turn from their wicked ways, I will hear from heaven and will forgive their sins and heal their land.

2 Chronicles 7:14 NLT

All of us (even "almost perfect" grandparents) have made mistakes, sometimes *big* mistakes. And when we fall short of our own expectations, or God's, we may experience intense feelings of guilt. But God has an answer for the guilt we feel. That answer, of course, is His forgiveness. When we confess our mistakes, if we learn from them, and if we stop repeating them, then we have every right to forgive ourselves.

Are you troubled by feelings of guilt or regret? If so, you must put yourself back on the right path (by putting an end to any residual misbehavior), and you must ask your heavenly Father for His forgiveness. When you do, He will forgive you completely and without reservation. Then you must forgive yourself just as God has forgiven you: thoroughly and unconditionally.

God's presence is such a cleansing fire,
confession and repentance are always there.

Anne Ortlund

Your Growing Faith

We also, since the day we heard it, do not cease to pray for you, and to ask that you may be filled with the knowledge of His will in all wisdom and spiritual understanding.
Colossians 1:9 NKJV

Your relationship with God is ongoing; it unfolds day by day, and it offers countless opportunities to grow closer to Him. As each new day unfolds, you are confronted with a wide range of decisions: how you will behave, where you will direct your thoughts, with whom you will associate, and what or whom you will choose to worship. These choices, along with many others like them, are yours and yours alone. How you choose determines how your relationship with God will unfold.

Are you continuing to grow both as a woman and as a grandmother, or are you satisfied with the current state of your spiritual health? Hopefully, you're determined to keep growing and growing. Your Creator deserves no less, and neither, by the way, do you.

Slowly and surely, we learn the great secret of life, which is to know God.
Oswald Chambers

Consider the Possibilities

Give your burdens to the LORD,
and he will take care of you.
He will not permit the godly to slip and fall.
Psalm 55:22 NLT

All of us face difficult days. Sometimes even the most optimistic grandmoms can become discouraged, and you are no exception. If you find yourself enduring difficult circumstances, perhaps it's time for an extreme intellectual makeover—perhaps it's time to focus more on your strengths and opportunities and less on the challenges that confront you. And one more thing: perhaps it's time to put a little more faith in God.

Every day, including this one, is brimming with possibilities. Every day is filled with opportunities to grow, to serve, and to share. But if you are entangled in a web of negativity, you may overlook the blessings that God has scattered along your path. So don't give in to pessimism, to doubt, or to cynicism. Instead, keep your eyes upon the possibilities, fix your heart upon the Creator, do your best, and let Him handle the rest.

In God's economy, whether He is making a flower or a human soul, nothing ever comes to nothing. The losses are His way of accomplishing the gains.
Elisabeth Elliot

The Language Our Kids Should Hear

Watch the way you talk. Let nothing foul or dirty come out of your mouth. Say only what helps, each word a gift.

Ephesians 4:29 MSG

The popularity of unseemly language is at an all-time high, and the trend is on the rise. Everywhere we turn, or so it seems, we're confronted with words (and images) that are inappropriate for grownups, not to mention kids.

So what's a grandmother to do? Well, you can't raise your family in a convent, but what you can do is this: (1) make sure that your family never hears you say something that you wouldn't want them to repeat; (2) make sure adults and children alike understand that your home is a profanity-free zone; and (3) don't allow inappropriate television shows, commercials, or movies to appear on your TV screen.

When you do these things, you'll make your house a small island of civility amid a sea of bad taste. You can't change the world, but you can control what is seen and said in your own home . . . and you should.

We will always experience regret when we live for the moment and do not weigh our words and deeds before we give them life.

Lisa Bevere

Church Matters

*I was glad when they said to me,
"Let us go to the house of the LORD."*
Psalm 122:1 NLT

The Bible teaches that we should worship God in our hearts and in community with other believers. We have clear instructions to "feed the church of God" (where church = people) and to worship our Creator in the presence of others. Yet it's not always easy for busy grandparents to find the time to become actively involved in a church.

We live in a world that is teeming with temptations and distractions. Our challenge, of course, is to ensure that we rise above the challenges of everyday life. We do so when we make God the central focus of our lives. One way that we remain faithful to the Creator is through the practice of regular, purposeful worship with our families. When we worship the Father faithfully, fervently, and frequently, we are blessed and so are our children and our grandchildren.

*Our churches are meant to be havens where
the caste rules of the world do not apply.*
Beth Moore

First Things First

First pay attention to me, and then relax.
Now you can take it easy—you're in good hands.
Proverbs 1:33 MSG

"First things first." These words are easy to speak but hard to put into practice. For busy women living in a demanding world, placing first things first can be difficult indeed. Why? Because so many people are expecting so many things from you!

If you're having trouble prioritizing your day, perhaps you've been trying to organize your life according to your own plans, not God's. A better strategy, of course, is to take your daily obligations and place them in the hands of the One who created you. To do so, you must prioritize your day according to God's commandments, and you must seek His will and His wisdom in all matters. Then, Grandmom, you can face the day with the assurance that the same God who created our universe out of nothingness will help you place first things first in your own life.

Oh, that we might discern the will of God, surrender to
His calling, resign the masses of activities,
and do a few things well.
What a legacy that would be for our children.
Beth Moore

God's Comfort

*Praise be to the God and Father of our Lord Jesus Christ.
God is the Father who is full of mercy and all comfort.
He comforts us every time we have trouble,
so when others have trouble, we can comfort them
with the same comfort God gives us.*

2 Corinthians 1:3–4 NCV

We live in a world that is, at times, a frightening place. We live in a world that is, at times, a discouraging place. We live in a world where life-changing losses can be so painful and so profound that it seems we will never recover. But with God's help, and with the help of encouraging family members and friends, we can recover.

During the darker days of life, we are wise to remember that God is with us always and that He offers us comfort, assurance, and peace—our task, of course, is to accept these gifts.

When we trust in God's promises, the world becomes a less frightening place. With God's comfort and His love in our hearts, we can tackle our problems with courage, determination, and faith.

*When I am criticized, injured, or afraid,
there is a Father who is ready to comfort me.*
Max Lucado

How Many Times?

*Peter came to Him and said, "Lord, how many times
could my brother sin against me and I forgive him?
As many as seven times?" "I tell you, not as many as
seven," Jesus said to him, "but 70 times seven."*
Matthew 18:21–22 HCSB

How often must we forgive our family members and friends? More times than we can count. Our children (and their children) are precious but imperfect; so are our spouses and our friends. So we must, on occasion, forgive those who have injured us; to do otherwise is to disobey God.

So here's a challenge for you, Grandmother: if there exists even one person, alive or dead, whom you have not forgiven (and that includes yourself), follow God's commandment and His will for your life—forgive. Regret and bitterness are not part of God's plan for your life. Forgiveness is.

*How often should you forgive the other person? Only as
many times as you want God to forgive you!*
Marie T. Freeman

Patience Pays

Patience is better than pride.
Ecclesiastes 7:8 NLT

The rigors of parenting and grandparenting can test the patience of the most mild-mannered men and women. After all, even the most mannerly children may, on occasion, do things that worry us or confuse us or anger us. Why? Because they are children and because they are human.

As loving parents and grandparents, we must be patient with our kids' shortcomings (just as they, too, must be patient with ours). Why? Because sometimes, patience is the price we pay for being responsible adults.

So today, Grandmother, do yourself and your loved ones this favor: be patient with everybody, starting with the woman you see when you look in the mirror. And while you're at it, be sure to be equally patient with all those folks you see when you look through your family photo album.

Waiting is an essential part of spiritual discipline.
It can be the ultimate test of faith.
Anne Graham Lotz

Who Rules?

You shall have no other gods before Me.
Exodus 20:3 NKJV

Who rules your heart? Is it God, or is it something else? Have you given God your heart, your soul, your talents, and your time, or have you formed the unfortunate habit of giving Him little more than a few hours each Sunday morning?

In the book of Exodus, God warns that we should place no gods before Him. Yet all too often, we place our Creator in second, third, or fourth place as we worship the gods of power, money, or prestige. When we unwittingly place our quest for status above our love for the Father, we must recognize our misplaced priorities and correct our behavior . . . or else.

Okay, Grandmother, here's today's big question: does God really rule your heart? Make certain that the honest answer to this question is a resounding yes. He deserves no less, and neither, for that matter, do you.

God has a genuine, passionate affection for each
of us and invites us to open our hearts to that love and
then return love to Him with deep sincerity.
Bill Hybels

The Thread of Generosity

If you have two coats, give one to the poor.
If you have food, share it with those who are hungry.
Luke 3:11 NLT

The thread of generosity is woven—completely and inextricably—into the very fabric of Christ's teachings. As He sent His disciples out to heal the sick and spread God's message of salvation, Jesus offered this guiding principle: "Freely you have received, freely give" (Matthew 10:8 NIV). The principle still applies.

Lisa Whelchel spoke for Christian women everywhere when she observed, "The Lord has abundantly blessed me all of my life. I'm not trying to pay Him back for all of His wonderful gifts; I just realize that He gave them to me to give away." All of us have been blessed, and all of us are called to share those blessings without reservation. So, make this pledge, Grandmother, and keep it: be a cheerful, generous, courageous giver. The world needs your help, and you need the spiritual rewards that will be yours when you share your possessions, your talents, and your time.

To show great love for God and our neighbor,
we need not do great things. It is how much love
we put in the doing that makes our offering something
beautiful for God.
Mother Teresa

July

Thank-You Hug for Grandmother

Dear Grandmother,

Thanks for the lessons about life. By your words and you're actions, you have taught us about love, discipline, hope, courage, responsibility, and more.

One of life's great ironies is that there is so much to learn and so little time. That's why we value the lessons you have taught us. You cared enough to teach, and we won't forget.

Your Bible and Your Family

The words of the LORD are pure words,
like silver tried in a furnace.
Psalm 12:6 NKJV

Are you sincerely seeking to discover God's will and follow it? If so, you and your loved ones must study His Word and follow His instructions. The words of Matthew 4:4 remind us that, "Man shall not live by bread alone, but by every word that proceeds from the mouth of God" (NKJV). So we should study the Bible and meditate upon its meaning for our lives. Otherwise, we deprive ourselves of a priceless gift from our Creator.

God's Word is, indeed, a one-of-a-kind treasure, and a passing acquaintance with the Good Book is insufficient for a thoughtful grandparent (like you) who seeks to obey God's Word and teach her family to do likewise. And that's good because no one should be asked to live by bread alone . . .

The Bible's durability is not found on earth; it is found in
heaven. For the millions who have tested its claims and
claimed its promises, there is but one answer—the Bible is
God's book and God's voice.
Max Lucado

July 2

Finding Serenity

*Those who love your law have great peace
and do not stumble.*
Psalm 119:165 NLT

The American theologian Reinhold Niebuhr composed a profoundly simple verse that came to be known as the Serenity Prayer: "God, grant me the serenity to accept the things I cannot change, the courage to change the things I can, and the wisdom to know the difference." Niebuhr's words are far easier for most mothers to recite than they are to live by. Why? Because most of us want life to unfold in accordance with our own wishes and timetables. But sometimes God has other plans for us and for our families.

When you trust God, you can be comforted in the knowledge that your Creator is both loving and wise and that He understands His plans perfectly well, even when you do not.

*Have courage for the great sorrows of life and patience
for the small ones, and when you have laboriously
accomplished your daily task,
go to sleep in peace. God is awake.*
Victor Hugo

July 3

God's Unfolding Plan for You

LORD, You are our Father; we are the clay,
and You are our potter;
we all are the work of Your hands.

Isaiah 64:8 HCSB

Each morning, as the sun rises in the east, you
welcome a new day, one that is filled to the brim
with opportunities, with possibilities, and with God.
As you contemplate God's blessings in your own life,
you should prayerfully seek His guidance for the day
ahead.

Discovering God's unfolding purpose for your life
is a daily journey, a journey guided by the teachings
of God's Holy Word. As you reflect upon God's
promises and upon the meaning that those promises
hold for you and your family, ask God to lead you
throughout the coming day. Let your heavenly Father
direct your steps; concentrate on what God wants
you to do now, and leave the distant future in hands
that are far more capable than your own: His hands.

*Life is not a journey you want to make
on autopilot.*
Paula Rinehart

Doing the Right Thing

*Now you must be holy in everything you do, just as God—
who chose you to be his children—is holy. For he himself
has said, "You must be holy because I am holy."*
1 Peter 1:15–16 NLT

When we do the right thing—and when we seek the companionship of people who do likewise—we reap the spiritual rewards that God intends for us to enjoy. When we live in accordance with the instructions of God's Word, He blesses us in ways that we cannot fully understand. Yet in some circles, doing the right thing seems to have gone out of style. What a pity.

Today, as you fulfill the many responsibilities of being a grandmother, hold fast to that which is good, and associate yourself with folks who behave themselves in like fashion. When you do, your good works will serve as a powerful example to your family and friends . . . and as a worthy offering to your Creator.

> *When we do what is right, we have
> contentment, peace, and happiness.*
> Beverly LaHaye

Discipline Matters

*Buy the truth and do not sell it; get wisdom,
discipline and understanding.*
Proverbs 23:23 NIV

God's Word makes it clear: we are instructed to
be disciplined, diligent, moderate, and mature.
But the world often tempts us, tempts our children,
and tempts our grandchildren to behave in other
ways. Everywhere we turn, or so it seems, we are faced
with powerful incentives to behave in ways that are
undisciplined, immoderate, and imprudent.

As a woman who has seen life and understands
life, you know God rewards diligence and righteousness just as certainly as He punishes laziness and misbehavior. And you know that God often teaches His
lessons sooner rather than later. So teach your children and grandchildren the fine art of self-discipline
. . . and just as important, teach them now.

*Real freedom means to welcome the responsibility
it brings, to welcome the God-control it requires,
to welcome the discipline that results,
to welcome the maturity it creates.*
Eugenia Price

Using Your Talents Now

*It is God who is working in you [enabling you] both
to will and to act for His good purpose.*
Philippians 2:13 HCSB

The old saying is both familiar and true: "What we are is God's gift to us; what we become is our gift to God." Each of us possesses special talents, gifted by God, that can be nurtured carefully or ignored totally. Our challenge, of course, is to use our abilities to the greatest extent possible and to use them in ways that honor our Savior.

Okay, Grandmother, are you really using your natural talents to make God's world a better place? If so, congratulations. But if you have gifts that you have not fully explored and developed, perhaps you need to have a chat with the One who gave you those gifts in the first place. Your talents are priceless treasures offered from your heavenly Father. Use them. Now. Before it's too late.

*Not everyone possesses boundless energy or
a conspicuous talent. We are not equally blessed with great
intellect or physical beauty or
emotional strength. But we have all been given
the same ability to be faithful.*
Gigi Graham Tchividjian

Being Strong Enough
(and Wise Enough) to Be Moderate

Moderation is better than muscle,
self-control better than political power.
Proverbs 16:32 MSG

As a woman who has lived long enough to know what works and what doesn't, you know that moderation and wisdom are traveling companions. If we are to live wisely and well, we must learn to temper our appetites, our desires, and our impulses. When we do, we are blessed, in part because God has created a world in which temperance is rewarded and intemperance is inevitably punished.

Would you like to improve your life? Then harness your appetites and restrain your impulses. Moderation is difficult, of course; it is especially difficult in a prosperous society such as ours. But the rewards of moderation are numerous and long-lasting . . . and you deserve those rewards. So why not start claiming them today.

Perhaps too much of everything
is as bad as too little.
Edna Ferber

Caring for Aging Parents?

*Let them first learn to do their duty to their
own family and to repay their parents or grandparents.
That pleases God.*

1 Timothy 5:4 NCV

If you're responsible, either directly or indirectly,
for the care of aging parents, you already know that
it's a challenging job at times. But you also know that
caring for your loved ones is not simply a duty; it is
also a responsibility and a privilege.

Caring for an elderly adult requires a mixture of
diplomacy, patience, insight, perseverance, gentleness, strength, compassion, wisdom, empathy, and,
most of all, an endless supply of love.

Sometimes the job of caring for aging parents
may seem like a thankless task, but it is not. Even
if your parents don't fully appreciate your sacrifices,
God does. And of this you may be certain: the Lord
will find surprising ways to reward your faithfulness
. . . now and in heaven.

*No matter how old they grow, some people never lose their
beauty. They merely move it from their faces into their
hearts.*

Barbara Johnson

Your Reasons to Rejoice

Keep your eyes focused on what is right,
and look straight ahead to what is good.

Proverbs 4:25 NCV

As a grandmother, you have many reasons to rejoice, starting, of course, with your kids and your kids' kids (not to mention the fact that dawn has broken on another day of life here on earth, and you're part of it). But when the demands of the day seem great, you may find yourself feeling exhausted, discouraged, or both. That's when you need a fresh supply of hope . . . and God is ready, willing, and able to supply it. Your task is to ask Him for it.

Are you an optimistic grandmom? Hopefully you understand the importance of maintaining a positive, can-do attitude—an attitude that pleases God.

As you face the challenges of the coming day, use God's Word as a tool for directing your thoughts. When you do, your attitude will be pleasing to God, pleasing to your friends, and pleasing to yourself.

I could go through this day oblivious
to the miracles all around me,
or I could tune in and "enjoy."

Gloria Gaither

A Grandchild Is . . .

Grandchildren are the crowning glory of the aged.
Proverbs 17:6 NLT

A little grandchild is a bundle of love wrapped up in possibilities. No wonder every grandbaby is the light of grandma's eyes. And no wonder so many women love spending time with their kid's kids. After all, grandmothers still have so much to teach, grandkids have so much to learn, and maybe, just maybe, the grandbabies (quite unlike their parents) haven't yet learned all there is to know!

So today, Grandmother, take time to thank the Creator, once again, for your loved ones. Your miraculous family, along with everything else in this miraculous universe, is a priceless gift on loan from the Father. And He most certainly deserves your praise and thanksgiving this day and every day.

The secret of life is to skip children
and go directly to grandchildren.
Mel Lazarus

God's Attentiveness

*The eyes of the LORD range throughout
the earth to show Himself strong for those
whose hearts are completely His.*
2 Chronicles 16:9 HCSB

God is not distant, and He is not disinterested. To the contrary, your heavenly Father is attentive to your needs. In fact, God knows precisely what you need and when you need it. But He still wants to talk with you, and if you're wise, you should want to talk to Him too.

Do you have questions that you simply can't answer? Ask for the guidance of your Creator. Do you sincerely seek the gift of everlasting love and eternal life? Accept God's gift of grace. Whatever your need, Grandmother, no matter how great or small, pray about it. Instead of waiting for mealtimes or bedtimes, pray always and never lose heart. And remember: God is here, and He's ready to talk with you now. So please don't make Him wait another moment.

*What a comfort to know that God is present
there in your life, available to meet every situation with
you, that you are never left to face
any problem alone.*
Vonette Bright

Understanding the Power of Faith

Blessed are all they that put their trust in him.
Psalm 2:12 KJV

Grandmothers, having seen it all more than once, understand the power of faith. As Grandmom knows, faith is the foundation upon which great lives are built. Faith is a gift we give ourselves, one that pays rich dividends in good times and hard times.

Faith, like a tender seedling, can be nurtured or neglected. When we nurture our faith through prayer, meditation, and worship, God blesses our lives and lifts our spirits. But when we fail to consult the Creator early and often, we do ourselves and our loved ones a disservice.

If your faith is being tested, reach out to your heavenly Father. With Him, all things are possible, and He stands ready to renew your strength whenever you're ready to ask. So ask. And keep asking. Today and every day.

Grandparents are honored for their years of wisdom and needed for their loving sensitivity. They have the privilege of reinforcing the godly lessons taught by parents and supplementing the spiritual nurture of the younger generation.
Dorothy Kelley Patterson

Your Source of Strength

Have you not known? Have you not heard?
The everlasting God, the LORD, the Creator of the ends of
the earth, neither faints nor is weary. His understanding is
unsearchable. He gives power to the weak,
and to those who have no might He increases strength.

Isaiah 40:28–29 NKJV

When the almighty and all-powerful God asks us to depend on Him for strength, why on earth would we not make our needs known to Him? The answer, of course, is that we have no reason to ignore the Creator and every reason to depend upon Him.

You have a specific purpose for the coming day, a purpose that only you can fulfill. And you can be sure that God will give you the strength to fulfill that purpose if you ask Him.

So today, Grandmother, as you make yourself available to your own tribe of high-maintenance grandkids (and even higher-maintenance grownups), don't try to do it alone. God is willing to help . . . and you should be willing to let Him.

We should talk to each other,
but it's when we talk together with God
that we are fully strengthened.

Annie Chapman

Not Anxiety, But Faith

> *Humble yourselves under the mighty hand of God,*
> *that He may exalt you at the proper time, casting all*
> *your anxiety on Him, because He cares for you.*
> 1 Peter 5:6–7 NASB

We live in a world that often breeds anxiety and fear. When we come face-to-face with tough times, we may fall prey to discouragement, doubt, or depression. But our Father in heaven has other plans. God has promised that we can lead lives of abundance, not anxiety. In fact, His Word instructs us to "be anxious for nothing" (Philippians 4:6 NASB). But how can we put our fears to rest? By taking those fears to God and leaving them there.

As you face the challenges of everyday living, do you find yourself becoming anxious, troubled, discouraged, or fearful? If so, turn every one of your concerns over to your heavenly Father. The same God who created the universe will comfort you if you ask Him . . . so ask Him and trust Him. And then watch in amazement as your anxieties melt into the warmth of His loving hands.

> *The beginning of anxiety is the end of faith,*
> *and the beginning of true faith is the end of anxiety.*
> George Müller

It Takes Time

The world with its lust is passing away,
but the one who does God's will remains forever.
1 John 2:17 HCSB

It takes time to build strong family ties . . . lots of time. Yet we live in a world where time seems to be an ever-shrinking commodity as we rush from place to place with seldom a moment to spare.

Has the busy pace of life robbed you of sufficient time with your loved ones? If so, it's time to fine-tune your priorities. And God can help.

When you make God a full partner in every aspect of your life, He will lead you along the proper path: His path. When you allow God to reign over your life, He will enrich your relationships and your life. So as you plan for the day ahead, make God's priorities your priorities. When you do, every other priority will have a tendency to fall neatly into place.

The connection between grandparents and grandchildren
is natural and second in emotional power only to the bond
between parent and child.
Arthur Kornhaber

The Power of Fellowship

*Don't you realize that all of you together are the temple of
God and that the Spirit of God lives in you?*

1 Corinthians 3:16 NLT

Every grandmother and her family—including you
and yours—deserve to be part of a community of
faith. Fellowship with others can make a powerful
contribution to the quality of your own life and to
the lives of your loved ones. Communal worship
enhances both community and worship.

Are you an active member of a Christian fellowship? Are you a builder of bridges within the four
walls of your church and outside it? And do you contribute to God's glory by contributing your time and
your talents? Hopefully so. The church is intended
to be a powerful tool for spreading God's message
and uplifting His children. And God intends for you
to be a fully contributing member. Your intentions
should be the same.

Be united with other Christians.
A wall with loose bricks is not good.
The bricks must be cemented together.

Corrie ten Boom

When Your Family Has Questions

The counsel of the LORD standeth for ever,
the thoughts of his heart to all generations.

Psalm 33:11 KJV

When you and your loved ones have questions that you simply can't answer, whom do you ask? When you face difficult decisions, to whom do you turn for counsel? To friends? To mentors? To family members? Or do you turn first to the ultimate source of wisdom? The answers to life's Big Questions start with God and His Word.

God's wisdom stands forever. God's Word is a light for every generation. Make it your light as well. Use the Bible as a compass for the next stage of your journey. Use it as the yardstick by which your behavior is measured. And as you carefully consult the pages of God's Word, prayerfully ask Him to reveal the wisdom that you need. When you and your family members take your concerns to God, He will not turn you away; He will, instead, offer answers that are tested and true. Your job is to ask, to listen, and to trust.

Be to the world a sign that while we as Christians
do not have all the answers,
we do know and care about the questions.

Billy Graham

Education Begins at Home

Train up a child in the way he should go,
and when he is old he will not depart from it.
Proverbs 22:6 NKJV

Responsible grandparents (like you) understand the value of education. That's why it's up to us to stress the importance of education. Here in the twenty-first century, education is no longer a luxury. It is a powerful tool and a shining light that snuffs out the darkness of ignorance and poverty. And when it comes to education, your family deserves nothing but the best.

Every child also deserves training in character building: lessons about honesty, responsibility, discipline, attitude, courtesy, dignity, self-worth, and respect for others. Certainly those lessons can and should be taught in school, but the ultimate training ground should be the home.

For grownups and kids alike, it's important to remember that school is always in session. So make a commitment to teach your grandchildren the important lessons as soon—and as often—as possible.

The task of the modern educator is not
to cut down jungles but to irrigate deserts.
C. S. Lewis

Who Needs Your Encouragement Today?

Careful words make for a careful life;
careless talk may ruin everything.

Proverbs 13:3 MSG

This world can be a difficult place, a place where many of our friends and family members are troubled by the inevitable challenges of everyday life. And since we can never be certain who needs our help, we should be careful to speak helpful words to everybody who crosses our paths.

In the book of Ephesians, Paul writes, "Do not let any unwholesome talk come out of your mouths, but only what is helpful for building others up according to their needs, that it may benefit those who listen" (4:29 NIV). Paul reminds us that when we choose our words carefully, we can have a powerful impact on those around us.

Today, Grandmother, be sure to share kind words, smiles, encouragement, and hugs with your family and friends. They need the encouragement . . . *and so do you.*

An effort made for the happiness of others
lifts us above ourselves.

Lydia Maria Child

Safe at Home

*Unless the LORD builds a house,
its builders labor over it in vain.*

Psalm 127:1 HCSB

A grandmother not only gives life to a family, she helps hold the family together. In doing so, she may perform a wide range of duties: mentor, chef, baby-sitter, counselor, and loan officer, to name but a few. Whew! It's a big job, but with God's help, savvy grandmoms have always been up to the task.

Certainly, in the life of every family, there are moments of frustration and disappointment. But, for grandparents who are lucky enough to experience the joys of caring for a close-knit, caring clan, the rewards far outweigh the frustrations. So today, Grandmother, take the time to offer up a special prayer of thanks for your family. After all, your loved ones are God's gifts to you. And in response to that gift, it's up to you to live—and to love—accordingly.

The woman is the heart of the home.

Mother Teresa

All Things Possible

All things are possible for the one who believes.
Mark 9:23 NCV

Are you genuinely excited about life and about the opportunities that God has placed before you and your family? Do you think that your Creator is a God of infinite possibilities, and are you energized by that thought? If so, you're a very wise grandmother. But if you've been living under a cloud of doubt, or if you're unsure whether or not to be excited about this day (and all the ones that follow it), God wants to have a little chat with you.

God's Word teaches us that all things are possible through Him. Do you believe that? If you do, then you can face the future with a mixture of excitement and delight.

God's power isn't limited; neither are your possibilities—and the sooner you realize it, the sooner you'll start building a better life for you and your loved ones.

Every intersection on the road of life
is an opportunity.
Duke Ellington

Finding the Right Balance

Take My yoke upon you and learn from Me, for I am gentle and lowly in heart, and you will find rest for your souls. For My yoke is easy and My burden is light.

Matthew 11:29–30 NKJV

Face facts: every woman's life is a delicate balancing act, a tightrope walk with overcommitment on one side and undercommitment on the other. And it's up to you to walk carefully on that rope, not falling prey to pride (which causes us to attempt too much) or to fear (which causes us to attempt too little).

God's Word promises us the possibility of abundance (John 10:10). And we are far more likely to experience that abundance when we lead balanced lives.

Okay, Grandmother, answer honestly: are you doing too much—or too little? If so, it's time to have a little chat with God. And if you listen carefully to His instructions, you will strive to achieve a more balanced life, a life that's right for you and your loved ones. When you do, everybody wins.

Live a balanced life—learn some and think some, and draw and paint, and sing and dance, and play and work every day some.

Robert Fulghum

The Spiritual Journey Continues

I've told you these things for a purpose: that my joy might be your joy, and your joy wholly mature.
John 15:11 MSG

As our lives unfold, we are constantly confronted with opportunities to learn, to explore, and to mature, and that's as it should be. The journey toward spiritual maturity is never a single destination; it is, instead, an ongoing process that continues moment by moment and day by day throughout every stage of life.

Every chapter of life has its own possibilities and its own challenges. If we're wise, we continue to seek God's guidance as each new stage unfolds. When we do so, we allow the Creator who made us to keep *remaking* us.

Today, focus your thoughts—and attune your heart—to the Father. He will teach you, He will shape you, and He will lead you along a path of His choosing. And if you're not sure of your next step, keep watching, keep listening, and keep praying. The answers will come.

If all struggles and sufferings were eliminated, the spirit would no more reach maturity than would the child.
Elisabeth Elliot

Positive Thoughts, Positive Prayers

Let all who take refuge in you be glad;
let them ever sing for joy.
Psalm 5:11 NIV

Wise grandmoms understand that thoughts have a tendency to transform themselves into reality. And so do prayers. So savvy grandmothers agree: a positive, prayerful attitude pays powerful dividends.

How will you direct your thoughts today? Will you focus on the silver linings or the clouds? Will you count your blessings or your inconveniences? Will you allow bitterness or cynicism or negativity or fear to infect your day, or will you make the conscious effort to infuse your mind with thoughts of praise and thanksgiving? The answer to these questions will determine, to a great extent, the tone of your day and the tone of your life. So choose your thoughts carefully. And be sure to guide them in the direction that is best for you and for your loved ones.

Let's please God by actively seeking, through prayer,
"peaceful and quiet lives" for ourselves,
our spouses, our children and grandchildren,
our friends, and our nation.
Shirley Dobson

The Miracle of God's Creation

*When I look at the night sky and see the work of your
fingers—the moon and the stars you have set in place—
what are mortals that you should think of us,
mere humans that you should care for us?*

Psalm 8:3–4 NLT

When we consider God's glorious universe, we
marvel at the miracle of nature. The smallest
seedlings and grandest stars are all parts of God's
infinite creation. God has placed His handiwork
on display for all to see, and if we are wise, we will
make time each day to celebrate the world that
surrounds us.

Today, as you fulfill the demands of everyday life,
pause to consider the majesty of heaven and earth. It
is as miraculous as it is beautiful, as incomprehensible
as it is breathtaking.

The psalmist reminds us that the heavens are a
declaration of God's glory. May we never cease to
praise the Father for a universe that stands as an
awesome testimony to His presence and His power.

*It is impossible for me to look at the heavens at night
without realizing there had to be a Creator.*

Ruth Bell Graham

Relationships According to God

Regarding life together and getting along with each other,
you don't need me to tell you what to do.
You're God-taught in these matters. Just love one another!
1 Thessalonians 4:9 MSG

As we travel along life's road, we build lifelong relationships with a small, dear circle of family and friends. One important way to build and maintain healthy relationships is by following the advice that can be found in God's Instruction Manual (also known as the Holy Bible).

Healthy relationships are built upon honesty, compassion, responsible behavior, trust, and optimism. Healthy relationships are built upon the Golden Rule. Healthy relationships are built upon sharing and caring. All of these principles are found time and time again in God's Word.

So the next time you're wondering how to treat a friend or family member, pull out your Bible and start reading. The answers you need can be found on those pages . . . your job is to find the answers—God's answers—and apply them to your relationships.

The truth of the Gospel is intended to free us to love God
and others with our whole heart.
John Eldredge

Learning to Accept the Past

*I do not consider myself to have taken hold of it.
But one thing I do: forgetting what is behind and reaching
forward to what is ahead, I pursue as my goal the prize
promised by God's heavenly call in Christ Jesus.*
Philippians 3:13–14 NIV

Has a tragedy left you angry at the world and disappointed with God? If so, it's time to accept the unchangeable past and to have faith in the promise of tomorrow. It's time to trust God completely, and it's time to reclaim the peace—His peace—that can and should be yours.

On occasion you and your family members will be confronted with situations that you simply don't understand. But God does. And He has a reason for everything He does.

God doesn't explain Himself in ways that we, as mortals with limited insight and clouded vision, can comprehend. So instead of understanding every aspect of God's unfolding plan for our lives and our universe, we must be satisfied to trust Him completely. We cannot know God's motivations, nor can we understand His actions. We can, however, trust Him, and we must.

*God whispers to us in our pleasures,
speaks in our conscience, but shouts in our pain.*
C. S. Lewis

Never "Just" a Grandmom

Mighty waters cannot extinguish love;
rivers cannot sweep it away.
Song of Songs 8:7 HCSB

One grandmother described herself this way: "I'm just a grandmother." That's like saying, "I'm just an astronaut," or, "I'm just a supreme court justice." Being a grandmother is not just another job. It's one of the most important jobs in God's creation.

As a grandmother, you understand the critical importance of guiding your family with love, with discipline, with wisdom, and with the Father. You know that your overriding purpose is to care for your children and grandchildren. You know that the Creator will bless your handiwork if you dedicate it to His glory. And you know that through your children and grandchildren, you have the power to refashion eternity.

So, you're never "just a grandmother." You are a wise woman fulfilling one of the most important duties on planet earth . . . and please don't ever forget it!

One of the most precious responsibilities of grandparents is the sharing of faith from generation to generation.
Dorothy Kelley Patterson

Beyond the World's Wisdom

The wisdom of this world is foolishness in God's sight.
1 Corinthians 3:19 NIV

The world has its own brand of wisdom, one that is often wrong and sometimes dangerous. God, on the other hand, has a different brand of wisdom, a wisdom that will never lead you astray.

Where will you place your trust today? Will you trust in the wisdom of fallible men and women, or will you place your faith in God's perfect wisdom? Your answer to this question will determine the direction of your day, the mood of your family, and the quality of your decisions.

As a loving grandparent, you're vitally interested in making good decisions for your family. God is vitally interested too. When you talk to Him early and often, your decisions will be sound and your family will be blessed.

The process of living seems to consist in coming to realize
truths so ancient and simple that,
if stated, they sound like barren platitudes.
They cannot sound otherwise to those who have not
had the relevant experience: that is why there is no real
teaching of such truths possible and
every generation starts from scratch.
C. S. Lewis

The Heart of a Servant

*Each one of us needs to look after the good of the people
around us, asking ourselves, "How can I help?"
That's exactly what Jesus did. He didn't make it easy for
himself by avoiding people's troubles, but waded right in
and helped out. "I took on the troubles of the troubled,"
is the way Scripture puts it.*

Romans 15:2–3 MSG

We live in a world that glorifies power, prestige, fame, and money. But the words of Jesus teach us that the most esteemed men and women in this world are not the self-congratulatory leaders of society but are instead the humblest of servants.

Today, Grandmother, find a need and fill it . . . humbly. Lend a helping hand . . . anonymously. Share a word of kindness . . . with quiet sincerity. As you go about your daily activities, remember that Jesus made Himself a servant, and you, as a caring grandparent and a responsible member of your community, must do no less.

*So many times we say that we can't serve God because we
aren't whatever is needed.
We're not talented enough or smart enough or whatever.
But if you are in covenant with Jesus Christ, He is
responsible for covering
your weaknesses, for being your strength.
He will give you His abilities for your disabilities!*

Kay Arthur

Trust the Shepherd

The LORD is my shepherd; I shall not want.
He makes me to lie down in green pastures;
He leads me beside the still waters. He restores my soul.
Psalm 23:1–3 NKJV

The beautiful words of the Twenty-third Psalm teach us that God is like a watchful shepherd caring for His flock, a flock that includes you. You and your family are precious in the eyes of God—you are His priceless creation, made in His image and protected by Him. God watches over you, and you need never be afraid. But sometimes fear has a way of slipping into the minds and hearts of even the most devout grandmoms—and you are no exception.

As a concerned grandparent, you know from firsthand experience that life is not always easy. But as a recipient of God's grace, you also know that you are protected by a loving heavenly Father.

Today, trust God's promises. And place your life in His hands. He is your Shepherd today and throughout eternity. Trust the Shepherd.

Thou art my Counselor, my Pattern, and my Guide, and
Thou my Shepherd art.
Issac Watts

August

Thank-You Hug for Grandmother

Dear Grandmother,

Thanks for your care, your concern, your help, and your kindness. Even in your busiest moments, you always made time for our family. Through your words and deeds, you have taught us a lesson that will last a lifetime: the power of compassion. And we will forever be grateful.

Prayer Changes Everything, Including You

*If you believe, you will receive
whatever you ask for in prayer.*
Matthew 21:22 HCSB

Is prayer an integral part of your daily life, or is it a hit-or-miss habit? Do you "pray without ceasing," or is prayer an afterthought? As you consider the role that prayer currently plays in your life—and the role that you think it should play—remember that the quality of your spiritual life is inevitably related to the quality of your prayer life.

Prayer changes things and it changes you. So, Grandmother, don't worry about your day, your future, or your next decision; just pray about these things, and leave the rest up to God. Don't limit your prayers to meals or to bedtime. Pray often about things great and small. God is listening, and He wants to hear from you. Now.

*God insists that we ask, not because He needs
to know our situation, but because we need
the spiritual discipline of asking.*
Catherine Marshall

Cheerfulness Is a Gift

A cheerful look brings joy to the heart,
and good news gives health to the bones.
Proverbs 15:30 NIV

Cheerfulness is a gift that you give to others and to yourself. And it's only right that you should be cheerful. After all, when you pause long enough to count your blessings (which start, of course, with your family), you will soon realize that you have many reasons to celebrate life with joy in your heart and a smile on your face.

Yet sometimes, even if you're the most upbeat grandmother on the block, you may be plagued by feelings of ill temper or frustration (who isn't?). Yet even then, you shouldn't allow negative emotions to go unchecked. Instead, you should catch your breath, cool your heals, recount your blessings, and try to cheer somebody up. When you do, you'll discover that good cheer is like honey: it's hard to spread it around without getting a little on yourself.

Cheerfulness prepares a glorious mind for all
the noblest acts of religion—love, adoration,
praise, and every union with our God.
St. Elizabeth Ann Seton

Do Something

Are there those among you who are truly wise and understanding? Then they should show it by living right and doing good things with a gentleness that comes from wisdom.
James 3:13 NCV

Grandmother, are you facing a big job or a particularly difficult task? If so, the most appropriate day to begin tackling that task is today.

Perhaps your challenges are simply too big to solve in a single sitting. But just because you can't solve everything doesn't mean that you should do nothing. Even small, incremental improvements are still improvements. Besides, once you get started solving your problems, you're likely to build momentum. And maybe, just maybe, the task at hand won't turn out to be as prickly as you first feared.

So today, Grandmother, as a favor to yourself and as a way of breaking the bonds of procrastination, do something to make your situation better. Even a small step in the right direction is still a step in the right direction. And a small step is far, far better than no step at all.

You must do the thing you think you cannot do.
Eleanor Roosevelt

Starting Your Day with God

*Morning by morning he wakens me and opens my
understanding to his will. The Sovereign LORD
has spoken to me, and I have listened.*

Isaiah 50:4–5 NLT

If you ever find that you're simply "too busy" for a daily chat with your Father in heaven, it's time to take a long, hard look at your priorities and your values. Each day has 1,440 minutes—do you value your relationship with God enough to spend a few of those minutes with Him? He deserves that much of your time and more—is He receiving it from you? Hopefully so.

As you consider your plans for the day ahead, Grandmother, here's a tip: organize your life around this simple principle: "God first." When you place your Creator where He belongs—at the very center of your day and your life—the rest of your priorities will fall into place.

*The moment you wake up each morning, all your wishes
and hopes for the day rush at you like wild animals. And
the first job each morning consists in shoving it all back;
in listening to that other voice, taking that other point of
view, letting that other, larger, stronger, quieter life coming
flowing in.*

C. S. Lewis

Opportunities to Encourage

*Encourage each other and give each other strength,
just as you are doing now.*

1 Thessalonians 5:11 NCV

Here's a question, Grandmother, that only you can answer: during a typical day, how many opportunities will you have to encourage your family and friends? Unless you're living on a deserted island, the answer is "a lot!" And here's a follow-up question: how often do you take advantage of those opportunities? Hopefully, the answer to question number two is "more often than not."

Whether you realize it or not, you're surrounded by people who need an encouraging word, a helping hand, a heartfelt prayer, a smile, a hug, or a good old-fashioned pat on the back. And every time you encourage one of these folks, you'll be doing God's will by obeying God's Word. So with no further ado, let the encouragement begin.

*My special friends, who know me so well
and love me anyway,
give me daily encouragement to keep on.*
Emilie Barnes

Loving the Kids and Teaching Them

Teach them to your children, talking about them when you sit in your house and when you walk along the road, when you lie down and when you get up.
Deuteronomy 11:19 HCSB

Every child is different, and every grandchild is different. But every child is similar in this respect: he or she is a priceless gift from the Father above. And with the Father's gift comes very real responsibilities for moms, for dads, and for grandparents.

Wise grandparents never forget they serve as the family's mentors, historians, teachers, standard bearers, and moral authorities. And the very best grandparents carry out their responsibilities with love, with kindness, with generosity, and with God.

Our children and grandchildren are our most precious resources. Every child is God's child. May we behave ourselves—and teach our children—accordingly.

Let us look upon our children;
let us love them and train them as children
of the covenant and children of the promise.
These are the children of God.
Andrew Murray

Do It Now

*Remember this: the person who sows sparingly
will also reap sparingly, and the person who sows
generously will also reap generously.*

2 Corinthians 9:6 HCSB

If you'd like another simple prescription for finding—and keeping—happiness, here it is: learn to do first things first, and learn to do them sooner rather than later.

Are you in the habit of doing what needs to be done when it needs to be done, or are you a dues-paying member of the Procrastinator's Club? If you've acquired the habit of doing your most important work first (even if you'd rather be doing something else), congratulations! But if you find yourself putting off all those unpleasant tasks until later (or never), it's time to think about the consequences of your behavior.

You can free yourself from the emotional quicksand by paying less attention to your fears and more attention to your responsibilities. So when you're faced with an unpleasant responsibility, don't spend endless hours fretting over it. Simply seek God's counsel and get busy. When you do, you will be richly rewarded because of your willingness to act.

All that is necessary to break the spell of inertia and frustration is this: Act as if it were impossible to fail.

Dorothea Brande

When the Answer Is No

Trust in the LORD with all your heart;
do not depend on your own understanding.
Proverbs 3:5 NLT

God answers our prayers. What God does not do is this: He does not always answer our prayers as soon as we might like, and He does not always answer our prayers by saying yes. God isn't an order taker, and He's not some sort of cosmic vending machine. Sometimes—even when we want something very badly—our loving heavenly Father responds to our requests by saying no, and we must accept His answer, even if we don't understand it.

God answers prayers not only according to our wishes but also according to His master plan. We cannot know that plan, but we can know the Planner . . . and we must trust His wisdom, His righteousness, and His love. Always.

Let's never forget that some of God's greatest mercies are
His refusals. He says no in order that
He may, in some way we cannot imagine, say yes.
All His ways with us are merciful.
His meaning is always love.
Elisabeth Elliot

Embracing the Aging Process

Gray hair is a glorious crown;
it is found in the way of righteousness.
Proverbs 16:31 HCSB

We live in a society that glorifies youth. The messages that we receive from the media are unrelenting: We are told that we must do everything within our power to retain youthful values and a youthful appearance. The goal, we are told, is to remain "forever young"—yet this goal is not only unrealistic, but it is also unworthy of women who understand what genuine beauty is, and what it isn't.

When it comes to health and beauty, you should focus more on health than on beauty. In fact, when you take care of your physical, spiritual, and mental health, your appearance will tend to take care of itself. And remember: God loves you during every stage of life—so embrace the aging process for what it is: an opportunity to grow closer to your loved ones and to your Creator.

It is magnificent to grow old, if one keeps young.
Harry Emerson Fosdick

Taking the Right Kinds of Risk

Be sure to stay busy and plant a variety of crops,
for you never know which will grow—perhaps they all will.
Ecclesiastes 11:6 NLT

As we consider the uncertainties of the future, we are confronted with a powerful temptation: the temptation to play it safe. Unwilling to move mountains, we fret over molehills. Unwilling to entertain great hopes for the tomorrow, we focus on the unfairness of the today. Unwilling to trust God completely, we take timid half steps when God intends that we make giant leaps. And we may, quite unintentionally, encourage our children and grandchildren to do likewise.

Today, ask God for the courage to step beyond the boundaries of your doubts. Ask Him to guide you to a place where you can realize your full potential—a place where you are freed from the fear of failure. And while you're at it, ask Him to give your loved ones the wisdom and the courage to do the same. Don't ask God to lead you to a "safe" place; ask Him to lead you to the "right" place . . . and remember: those two places are seldom the same.

To have failed is to own more wisdom, understanding, and
experience than do those who sit on life's sidelines playing
it safe.
Susan Lenzkes

Keeping Up?

Where your treasure is, there your heart will be also.
Luke 12:34 NKJV

As a member in good standing in this highly competitive twenty-first-century world, you know that the demands and expectations of everyday living can seem burdensome, even overwhelming at times. Keeping up with the Joneses can become a full-time job if you let it. A better strategy, of course, is to stop trying to please the neighbors and to concentrate, instead, upon pleasing God.

Perhaps you have high aspirations for yourself and your family; if so, congratulations! You're willing to dream big dreams, and that's a very good thing. But as you consider your life's purpose, don't allow your quest for excellence to interfere with the spiritual journey that God has planned for you and yours.

Whom will you try to please today, your Creator . . . or the Joneses? The answer should be obvious.

The best things in life aren't things.
Art Buchwald

When Mistakes Happen

*He whose ear listens to the life-giving reproof
will dwell among the wise.*
Proverbs 15:31 NASB

Even "nearly perfect" grandparents are far from perfect. And, without question, their children and grandchildren are imperfect as well. Yes, we are all imperfect members of imperfect families, and, as a result, mistakes are bound to happen.

Has someone in your family experienced a recent setback? If so, it's time to start looking for the lesson that God is trying to teach. It's time to learn what needs to be learned, change what needs to be changed, and move on.

You and your loved ones should view mistakes as opportunities to reassess God's will for your lives. And while you're at it, you should consider life's inevitable disappointments to be powerful opportunities to learn more—more about yourselves, more about your circumstances, and more about your world.

*Mature people are not emotionally and spiritually
devastated by every mistake they make.
They are able to maintain some kind
of balance in their lives.*
Joyce Meyer

Pray Hard, Work Hard

Each tree is known by its own fruit.
Luke 6:44 HCSB

The old adage is both familiar and true: we must pray as if everything depended upon God but work as if everything depended upon us. Yet sometimes, when we are weary and discouraged, we may allow our worries to sap our energy and our hope. God has other intentions. God intends that we pray for things, and He intends that we be willing to work for the things that we pray for. More important, God intends that our work should become His work.

Are you a grandmother who is working hard for your family and for your God? If so, you can expect your heavenly Father to bring forth a rich harvest.

And if you have concerns about the inevitable challenges of everyday living, take those concerns to God in prayer. He will guide your steps, He will steady your hand, He will calm your fears, and He will reward your efforts.

Can anything be sadder than work unfinished?
Yes: work never begun.
Christina Rossetti

Looking to Jesus

*This is the secret: Christ lives in you, and this
is your assurance that you will share in his glory.*
Colossians 1:27 NLT

Hannah Whitall Smith spoke to Christians of every generation when she advised, "Keep your face upturned to Christ as the flowers do to the sun. Look, and your soul shall live and grow." How true. When we turn our hearts to Jesus, we receive His blessings, His peace, and His grace.

Jesus belongs at the very center of our lives. And when we put Him there with our thoughts, our prayers, and our deeds, we are blessed. As we look upward to God's Son, we discover a genuine sense of serenity and abundance that the world, by itself, simply cannot provide. So today, Grandmother, share the story of Christ's love with a family member or friend. It's a message that someone very near you desperately needs to hear.

*When you can't see him, trust him.
Jesus is closer than you ever dreamed.*
Max Lucado

The Futility of Worry

Worry is a heavy load.
Proverbs 12:25 NCV

Because we have the ability to think, we also have the ability to worry. Even the most optimistic among us are plagued by occasional periods of discouragement and doubt. More often than not, our worries stem from our failure to focus on a priceless gift from God: the profound, precious, present moment. Instead of thanking God for the blessings of this day, we stew about the unfairness of the past, or we agonize about the uncertainty of the future.

When you stop to think about it, you'll probably agree that most of the things you worry about never come to pass. In fact, worry is simply the mind's way of cluttering up today's opportunities with memories of troubles that have already passed—or fears about troubles that may never come. So focus on this day, and turn your worries over to a Power greater than yourself. Spend your time and energy solving the problems you can fix today . . . while trusting God to do the rest.

I've read the last page of the Bible.
It's all going to turn out all right.
Billy Graham

Beyond Our Obstacles

*Even though good people may be bothered
by trouble seven times, they are never defeated.*

Proverbs 24:16 NCV

The occasional disappointments and failures of life are inevitable. Such setbacks are simply the price that we must occasionally pay for our willingness to take risks as we pursue our goals. But even when we encounter bitter disappointments, we must never lose faith.

As grandparents, we are far from perfect. And, without question, our children and grandchildren are imperfect as well. When we make mistakes, we must correct them and learn from them. And when our families make mistakes, we must help them do likewise.

Have you or one of your family members made a small error, a medium-sized mistake, or a big-time blunder? If so, remember that God's love is permanent, but for hardworking folks (like you) failure never is.

*How beautiful it is to learn that grace isn't fragile, and
that in the family of God
we can fail and not be a failure.*

Gloria Gaither

When Your Conscience Speaks

The Lord says, "I will make you wise
and show you where to go."

Psalm 32:8 NCV

Hey, Grandmother, when God speaks through that small, quiet voice that He has placed in your heart, are you ready and willing to listen? Hopefully so; after all, God has equipped you with a conscience and a clear sense of right and wrong, and He intends for you to use it.

But sometimes, especially in times of crisis, it's hard to trust your own insights because your inner voice—God's internal guidance system—can be drowned out by fear, worry, anxiety, or confusion.

If you're facing a difficult question or an important decision, your most trusted advisor may very well be that small, still voice that God has placed within you. So listen intently to your conscience, and pay careful attention to the things you hear. God is probably trying to get His message through to you, but He may not be willing to shout.

One of the ways God has revealed Himself to us is in the
conscience. Conscience is God's lamp
within the human breast.

Billy Graham

Experiencing Spiritual Abundance

*My cup runneth over. Surely goodness and mercy shall
follow me all the days of my life: and I will dwell
in the house of the LORD for ever.*

Psalm 23:5–6 KJV

God does not promise us abundance. He promises that we "might have life" and that we "might have it more abundantly" if we accept His grace, His blessings, and His Son (John 10:10 KJV). When we commit our hearts and our days to the One who created us, we experience spiritual abundance through the grace and sacrifice of His Son, Jesus. But when we focus our thoughts and energies not upon God's perfect will for our lives but instead upon our own unending assortment of earthly needs and desires, we inevitably forfeit the spiritual abundance that might otherwise be ours.

Today and every day, seek God's will for your life, and follow it. Today, turn your worries and your concerns over to your heavenly Father. Today, seek God's wisdom, follow His commandments, trust His judgment, and honor His Son. When you do, spiritual abundance will be yours, not just for this day, but for all eternity.

*The only way you can experience abundant life
is to surrender your plans to Him.*

Charles Stanley

August 19

The Trap of Pessimism

Why are you cast down, O my soul? And why are you disquieted within me? Hope in God; for I shall yet praise Him, the help of my countenance and my God.
Psalm 42:11 NKJV

Sometimes, despite our trust in God, we may fall into the spiritual traps of worry, frustration, anxiety, or sheer exhaustion, and our hearts become heavy. What's needed is plenty of rest, a large dose of perspective, and God's healing touch, but not necessarily in that order.

Pessimism is a trap—don't fall into it. Instead, make this promise to yourself and keep it: vow to be a hope-filled woman. Think optimistically about your life, your family, your friends, your faith, and your future. Trust your hopes, not your fears. Take time to celebrate God's glorious creation. And then, when you've filled your heart with hope and gladness, share your optimism with others. Your loved ones will be better for it, Grandmother, and so will you. But not necessarily in that order.

We never get anywhere—
nor do our conditions and circumstances change—
when we look at the dark side of life.
Mrs. Charles E. Cowman

Living in an Anxious World

*Better is a dry morsel and quietness with it
than a house full of feasting with strife.*

Proverbs 17:1 NASB

We live in a fast-paced, stress-inducing, anxiety-filled world that oftentimes seems to shift beneath our feet. During stressful times, trusting God can be more difficult, especially if we allow ourselves to become caught up in the incessant demands of a clamorous and anxious world.

When you feel stressed to the breaking point—and you will—return your thoughts to God's love and God's promises. And as you confront the challenges of everyday living, turn all of your concerns over to your heavenly Father.

The same God who created the universe will comfort and guide you when you ask Him. Ask Him often. And then, Grandmother, watch in quiet amazement as your anxieties melt into the warmth of His loving hands.

*The greatest weapon against stress is our ability to choose
one thought over another.*

William James

Finding Contentment

> So then, we must pursue what promotes peace
> and what builds up one another.
>
> Romans 14:19 HCSB

Where can you find contentment? Is it a result of wealth or power or beauty or fame? Hardly. Genuine contentment springs from a peaceful spirit, a clear conscience, and a loving heart (like yours!).

Our modern world seems preoccupied with the search for happiness. We are bombarded with messages telling us that happiness depends upon the acquisition of material possessions. These messages are false. Enduring peace is not the result of our acquisitions; it is the inevitable result of our dispositions. If we don't find contentment within ourselves, we will never find it outside ourselves.

Thus the search for contentment is an internal quest, an exploration of the heart, mind, and soul. You can find contentment, indeed you will find it—if you simply look in the right places. And the best time to start looking in those places is now.

> *When we do what is right, we have contentment, peace,*
> *and happiness.*
> Beverly LaHaye

The Right to Say No

*In a race, everyone runs but only one person gets
first prize. . . . To win the contest you must deny yourselves
many things that would keep you from doing your best.*

1 Corinthians 9:24–25 TLB

Okay, Grandmother, you know all too well how many people are making demands upon your time. If you're like most grandmothers, you've got plenty of people pulling you in lots of directions, starting, of course, with your family—but not ending there.

Perhaps you also have additional responsibilities at work or at church. Maybe you're active in community affairs, or maybe you are involved in any of a hundred other activities that gobble up big portions of your day. If so, you'll need to be sure that you know when to say enough is enough.

When it comes to squeezing more and more obligations onto your daily to-do list, you have the right to say no when you simply don't have the time, the energy, or the desire to do the job. And if you're wise, you'll learn so say no as often as necessary . . . or else!

*Learn to say no gracefully; resist the temptation to chase
after more pleasure, more hobbies,
and more social entanglements.*

James Dobson

August 23

The Right Kind of Fear

The fear of the LORD is the beginning of knowledge,
but fools despise wisdom and discipline.

Proverbs 1:7 NIV

Do you have a healthy, fearful respect for God's power? If so, you are wise. And because you are a thoughtful woman who has seen her fair share of life, you also understand that genuine wisdom begins with a profound appreciation for God's limitless power.

God praises humility and punishes pride. That's why God's greatest servants will always be those humble men and women who care less for their own glory and more for God's glory. In God's kingdom, the only way to achieve greatness is to shun it. And the only way to be wise is to understand these facts: God is great; He is all-knowing; and He is all-powerful. We must respect Him, and we must humbly obey His commandments, or we must accept the consequences of our misplaced pride.

The fear of God is the death of every other fear.

C. H. Spurgeon

Beyond the Temptations

Friend, don't go along with evil. Model the good.
The person who does good does God's work.
The person who does evil falsifies God,
doesn't know the first thing about God.

3 John 1:11 MSG

We are all born into a world that tries its hardest to push us and families away from God's will. Society, it seems, is causing pain and heartache in more ways than ever before. We, as mothers, must remain watchful and strong. And the good news is this: when it comes to fighting evil, we are never alone. God is always with us, and He gives us the power to resist temptation whenever we ask Him to give us strength.

In a letter to believers, Peter offered a stern warning: "Your adversary, the devil, prowls around like a roaring lion, seeking someone to devour" (1 Peter 5:8 NASB). As a thoughtful grandmother, you will take that warning seriously and encourage your loved ones to take it seriously too.

In the Garden of Gethsemane, Jesus went through agony
of soul in His efforts to resist the temptation to do what
He felt like doing rather than what
He knew was God's will for Him.

Joyce Meyer

When Change Is Painful

Nothing will be impossible with God.
Luke 1:37 HCSB

When life unfolds according to our wishes, or when we experience unexpected good fortune, we find it easy to praise God's plan. That's when we greet change with open arms. But sometimes the changes that we must endure are painful. When we struggle through the difficult days of life, as we must from time to time, we may ask ourselves, "Why me?" The answer, of course, is that God knows, but He isn't telling . . . yet.

Have you endured a difficult transition that has left your head spinning or your heart broken? If so, you have a clear choice to make: either you can cry and complain, or you can trust God and get busy fixing what's broken. The former is a formula for disaster; the latter is a formula for a well-lived life. So, Grandmother, make today the day when the fretting ceases and the fixing begins.

Often God shuts a door in our face
so that he can open the door
through which he wants us to go.
Catherine Marshall

Neighbors

Show family affection to one another with brotherly
love. Outdo one another in showing honor. Do not lack
diligence; be fervent in spirit; serve the Lord. Rejoice in
hope; be patient in affliction; be persistent in prayer.
Romans 12:10–12 HCSB

Neighbors. We know that we are instructed to love them, and yet there's so little time . . . and we're so busy. No matter. We are instructed to love our neighbors just as we love ourselves. In the Bible, we are not asked to love our neighbors, nor are we encouraged to do so. We are commanded to love them. Period.

This very day, Grandmother, you will encounter someone who needs a word of encouragement or a pat on the back or a helping hand or a heartfelt prayer. And if you don't reach out to that person, who will? If you don't take the time to understand the needs of your neighbors, who will? If you don't love your brothers and sisters, who will? So, today, Grandmother, look for a neighbor in need . . . and then do something to help. Father's orders.

A person who really cares about his or her neighbor, a
person who genuinely loves others,
is a person who bears witness to the truth.
Anne Graham Lotz

When We Don't Understand

Trust in the LORD with all your heart;
do not depend on your own understanding.
Seek his will in all you do, and he will direct your paths.
Proverbs 3:5–6 NLT

When our dreams come true and our plans prove successful, we find it easy to thank our Creator and trust His divine providence. But in times of sorrow or hardship, we may find ourselves questioning God's plans for our lives.

On occasion, you will confront circumstances that trouble you to the very core of your soul. It is during these difficult days that you must find the wisdom and the courage to trust your heavenly Father despite your circumstances.

Are you a grandmother who seeks God's blessings for yourself and your family? Then trust Him. Trust your heavenly Father day by day, moment by moment—in good times and in trying times. Then wait patiently for God's revelations . . . and prepare yourself for the abundance and peace that will most certainly be yours when you do.

The more we learn to receive and depend upon
His grace in deepening measure, the less anxious
we will be about what the future holds.
Cynthia Heald

Small Choices

Not my will, but thine, be done.
Luke 22:42 KJV

Each of us faces hundreds of small choices each day, choices that make up the fabric of daily life. When we align those choices with God's commandments, and when we align our lives with God's will, we receive His abundance, His peace, and His joy. But when we struggle against God's will for our lives—when we insist upon doing things our way, not God's way—we reap a less bountiful harvest.

Today, you'll face hundreds of small decisions; as you do, use God's Word as your guide. And while you're at it, Grandmother, pay careful attention to the small, quiet voice—your conscience—that God has placed in your heart. In matters great and small, seek the will of God, and trust Him. He will never lead you astray. Never.

Joy is not gush; joy is not mere jolliness.
Joy is perfect acquiescence, acceptance,
and rest in God's will, whatever comes.

Amy Carmichael

Obey and Be Blessed

Good people will have rich blessings,
but the wicked will be overwhelmed.
Proverbs 10:6 NCV

God has given us a guidebook for victorious living; it's called the Bible, and it contains thorough instructions, which, if followed, will bring us a wide array of rewards and blessings.

The Bible instructs us that a righteous life has many components: faith, honesty, generosity, love, kindness, humility, gratitude, and worship, to name but a few. And if we seek to please the Creator, we must, to the best of our abilities, live according to the principles contained in His Holy Word.

As a loving grandmother, you are keenly aware that God has entrusted you with a profound responsibility: caring for the needs of your family, including their spiritual needs. To fulfill that responsibility, you must study God's Word and live by it. When you do, your example will be a blessing not only to your loved ones, but also to generations yet unborn.

He doesn't need an abundance of words.
He doesn't need a dissertation about your life.
He just wants your attention.
He wants your heart.
Kathy Troccoli

The Other Side of Anger

Rash language cuts and maims,
but there is healing in the words of the wise.
Proverbs 12:18 MSG

Anger is a natural human emotion that is sometimes necessary and appropriate. Even Jesus became angry when confronted with the money-changers in the temple. Righteous indignation is an appropriate response to evil, but God does not intend that anger should rule our lives. Far from it. God intends that we turn away from anger whenever possible and forgive our neighbors as quickly as we can find it in our hearts to do so.

When you are tempted to lose your temper over the minor inconveniences of life, don't. Turn away from anger, hatred, bitterness, frustration, and regret. Be quick to forgive imperfections—other people's imperfections and your own. After all, you deserve the peace that can be yours when you proceed as quickly as possible to the other side of anger.

Anger breeds remorse in the heart,
discord in the home, bitterness in the community, and
confusion in the state.
Billy Graham

Walking with God

How happy is everyone who fears the Lord,
who walks in His ways!
Psalm 128:1 HCSB

As you take the next step in your life's journey, be sure that you're walking with God. Jesus called upon believers to walk with Him, and He promised them that He would teach them how to live wisely, how to live well, and how to live eternally.

Are you worried or anxious? Be confident in God's power. He will never desert you. Do you see no hope for the future? Be courageous and call upon God. He will protect you and then use you according to His purposes. Are you grieving? Know that God hears your suffering. He will comfort you and, in time, He will dry your tears. Are you confused? Listen to the quiet voice of your heavenly Father. He is not a God of confusion. Talk with Him; listen to Him; follow His commandments. He is steadfast, and He is your Protector . . . forever.

Waiting on God is the same as walking
with God toward exciting new rooms
of potential and service.
Susan Lenzkes

September

Thank-You Hug for Grandmother

Dear Grandmother,

Every family (including ours) needs positive role models. Thanks for being one. You have taught us some of life's most important lessons, not only by your words but also by your actions.

You weren't always perfect—nobody is—but when you did make mistakes, you corrected them, you moved on, and we learned.

Because of the example you've set, you are a powerful force for good in our home . . . and far

He Loves You

Praise the LORD, all nations! Glorify Him, all peoples!
For great is His faithful love to us;
the LORD's faithfulness endures forever. Hallelujah!
Psalm 117 HCSB

Because God's power is limitless, it is far beyond the comprehension of mortal minds. But even though we cannot fully understand the heart of God, we can be open to God's love.

God's ability to love is not burdened by temporal boundaries or by earthly limitations. The love that flows from the heart of God is infinite—and today presents yet another opportunity to celebrate that love.

Today, as you carve out quiet moments of thanksgiving and praise for your heavenly Father, open yourself to His presence and His love. He is here, waiting. His love is here, always.

You are a glorious creation, a unique individual, a beautiful example of God's handiwork. God's love for you is limitless. Accept that love, acknowledge it, and be grateful.

God does not love us because we are valuable.
We are valuable because God loves us.
Fulton J. Sheen

What to Do?

The lines of purpose in your lives never grow slack,
tightly tied as they are to your future
in heaven, kept taut by hope.
Colossians 1:5 MSG

"What on earth does God intend for me to do with the rest of my life?" It's an easy question to ask but, for many of us, a difficult question to answer. Why? Because God's purposes aren't always clear to us. Sometimes we wander aimlessly in a wilderness of our own making. And sometimes we struggle mightily against God in an unsuccessful attempt to find success and happiness through our own means, not His.

Sometimes God's intentions will be clear to you; other times God's plan will seem uncertain at best. But even on those difficult days when you are unsure which way to turn, you must never lose sight of these overriding facts: God created you for a reason; He has important work for you to do; and He's waiting patiently for you to do it.

The next step is up to you.

It's incredible to realize that what we do each day has
meaning in the big picture of God's plan.
Bill Hybels

The Beauty of Your Aspirations

Commit your works to the LORD,
and your thoughts will be established.
Proverbs 16:3 NKJV

As you take the next step in your life's journey, you should do so with feelings of hope and anticipation. After all, if you're a thoughtful woman and a thankful grandmother, you already have countless reasons to rejoice. But sometimes rejoicing may be the last thing on your mind. At times you may feel overwhelmed by the inevitable stresses or the occasional disappointments of everyday life. But for a thankful woman like you, any feelings of discouragement can—indeed should—be temporary.

The next time you become disheartened by the direction of your day or your life, ask God to help you count your blessings, not your hardships. And while you're talking to God, remember that even when the challenges of the day seem daunting, He remains steadfast. And so must you.

Far away in the sunshine are my highest aspirations. I may
not reach them, but I can look up
and see the beauty, believe in them,
and try to follow where they lead.
Louisa May Alcott

The Lessons of Tough Times

They won't be afraid of bad news;
their hearts are steady because they trust the Lord.
Psalm 112:7 NCV

In the midst of adversity, you may find it difficult to see the purpose of your suffering. Yet of this you can be sure: the times that try your soul are also the times that build your character. During the darker days of life, you can learn lessons that are impossible to learn during sunny, happier days. Times of adversity can—and should—be times of intense spiritual and personal growth.

The next time Old Man Trouble knocks on your door, remember that he has lessons to teach. So turn away Mr. Trouble as quickly as you can, but as you're doing so, don't forget to learn his lessons. And remember: the trouble with trouble isn't just the trouble it causes; it's also the trouble we cause ourselves if we ignore the things that trouble has to teach.

We should not be upset when unexpected
and upsetting things happen. God, in his wisdom, means
to make something of us which
we have not yet attained, and He is dealing
with us accordingly.
J. I. Packer

What's Really Important

Anyone trusting in his riches will fall,
but the righteous will flourish like foliage.
Proverbs 11:28 HCSB

In the demanding world in which we live, financial prosperity can be a good thing, but spiritual prosperity is profoundly more important. Yet our society leads us to believe otherwise. The world glorifies material possessions, personal fame, and physical beauty above all else; these things, of course, are totally unimportant to God. God sees the human heart, and that's what is important to Him.

As you establish your priorities for the coming day, remember this, Grandmother: the world will do everything it can to convince you that "things" are important. The world will tempt you to value fortune above faith and possessions above peace. God, on the other hand, will try to convince you that your relationship with Him is all-important. Trust God.

True contentment comes from godliness
in the heart, not from wealth in the hand.
Warren Wiersbe

September 6

Faith Works Miracles

We walk by faith, not by sight.
2 Corinthians 5:7 NKJV

When Mary McLeod Bethune was born in 1875 to parents who were former slaves, few could have guessed that she would change the face of American education. But she did. After teaching school for only five years, she founded the Daytona Normal and Industrial Institute for Negro Girls. Today that Florida school, now known as Bethune-Cookman College, continues its mission.

In the beginning, Mary McLeod Bethune operated on a shoestring. What was required was faith. Bethune once observed, "Without faith nothing is possible. With it, nothing is impossible." How right she was.

So the next time you come face-to-face with the illusion of impossibility, Grandmother, remember that Mary McLeod Bethune proved once and for all that faith is the foundation upon which great schools—and great miracles—are built.

Sometimes the very essence of faith is trusting God in the midst of things He knows good and well we cannot comprehend.
Beth Moore

The Blessings of Obedience

It is the LORD your God you must follow,
and him you must revere. Keep his commands
and obey him; serve him and hold fast to him.
Deuteronomy 13:4 NIV

We are sorely tempted to pick and choose which of God's commandments we will obey and which of His commandments we will discard. But the Bible clearly instructs us to do otherwise.

God's Word commands us to obey all of His laws, not just the ones that are easy or convenient. When we do, we are blessed by a loving heavenly Father.

Today, take every step of your journey with God as your traveling companion. Read His Word and obey His commandments. Support only those activities that further God's kingdom and your spiritual growth. Be an example of righteous living to your children, to your grandchildren, to your friends, to your neighbors, and to your community. Then reap the blessings that God has promised to all those who live according to His will and His Word.

Our obedience does not make God any bigger or better
than He already is. Anything God commands of us is
so that our joy may be full—the joy of seeing His glory
revealed to us and in us!
Beth Moore

Smile

> Jacob said, "For what a relief it is to see
> your friendly smile. It is like seeing the smile of God!"
> Genesis 33:10 NLT

A smile is nourishment for the heart, and laughter is medicine for the soul—but sometimes, amid the stresses of the day, we forget to take our medicine. Instead of viewing our world with a mixture of optimism and humor, we allow worries and distractions to rob us of the joy that God intends for our lives.

So the next time you find yourself dwelling upon the negatives of life, refocus your attention to things positive. The next time you find yourself falling prey to the blight of pessimism, stop yourself and turn your thoughts around. With a loving God as your protector, and with a loving family to support you, you're blessed now and forever.

So smile . . . beginning now!

> A smile is the light in the window of your face
> that tells people you're at home.
> Barbara Johnson

Judging Others

*When they continued to ask Jesus their question,
he raised up and said, "Anyone here who has never sinned
can throw the first stone at her."*

John 8:7 NCV

Okay, answer honestly: are you a woman who finds it easy to judge others? If so, you're not alone; we humans are often quick, too quick, in fact, to judge others. Yet in our better moments, we should remember that, in matters of judgment, God does not need (or want) our help in judging. Why? Because God is perfectly capable of judging the human heart . . . while we are not.

All of us have fallen short of God's laws, and none of us, therefore, is qualified to "cast the first stone." Thankfully, God has forgiven us, and we, too, must forgive others. Let us refrain, then, from judging our family members, our friends, and our loved ones. Instead, let us forgive them and love them in the same way that God has forgiven us and loves us.

*Here's a simple rule of thumb:
Don't judge other people more harshly
than you want God to judge you.*

Marie T. Freeman

Quality Time and Quantity Time

Teach us to number our days,
that we may gain a heart of wisdom.
Psalm 90:12 NKJV

Make no mistake: caring for your family requires time—lots of time. You've probably heard about "quality time" and "quantity time." Your family needs both. So as a responsible grandmother, you'll willingly invest large quantities of your time and energy in the care and nurturing of your clan.

While caring for your family, you can do your best to ensure that God remains squarely at the center of your household. When you do, God will bless you and yours in ways that you scarcely could have imagined.

So as you make plans for the day ahead, and as you think about how you're going to allocate your time, Grandmother, make sure that you're giving your clan both quality and quantity. They deserve it, and so do you.

The work of God is appointed.
There is always enough time
to do the will of God.
Elisabeth Elliot

Pleasing Whom?

Do you think I am trying to make people accept me?
No, God is the One I am trying to please.
Galatians 1:10 NCV

If you're like most people, you seek the admiration of your neighbors, your coworkers, and your family members. But the eagerness to please others should never overshadow your eagerness to please God. In every aspect of your life, pleasing your heavenly Father should come first.

Would you like a time-tested formula for successful living—a strategy that will enrich your own life and the lives of your loved ones? Here is a formula that is proven and true: seek God's approval first and other people's approval later. Does this sound too simple? Perhaps it is simple, but it is also the surest way to reap the marvelous riches that God has in store for you and yours.

When we are set free from the bondage of pleasing others,
when we are free from currying others' favor and others'
approval—then no one will be able to make us miserable or
dissatisfied. And then,
if we know we have pleased God,
contentment will be our consolation.
Kay Arthur

Grandparenting by Example

God-loyal people, living honest lives,
make it much easier for their children.
Proverbs 20:7 MSG

It would be very easy to teach our kids and grandkids everything they need to know about life if we could teach them with words alone. But we can't. They hear some of the things we say, but they watch everything we do.

As grandparents, we serve as unforgettable role models for our children and our grandchildren. The lives we lead and the choices we make should serve as enduring examples of the spiritual abundance that is available to all who worship God and obey His commandments.

So today, Grandmother, as you make the many choices that, taken together, form the tapestry of your life, remember that little eyes are watching . . . and so, for that matter, is God.

Grandparents are the living link
to the family's past.
Arthur Kornhaber

September 13

Power Supply

*Come to Me, all you who are weary and burdened,
and I will give you rest. All of you, take up My yoke and
learn from Me, because I am gentle and humble in heart,
and you will find rest for yourselves.
For My yoke is easy and My burden is light.*

Matthew 11:28–30 HCSB

Have you been trying to get through life using nothing but your own resources? If so, it's high time for a power boost. Are you weary, worried, fretful or fearful? If so, it's time to turn to a strength much greater than your own.

You have, at your fingertips, a power supply that never fails. It is, of course, the power that flows from God, and He is always willing to share His strength with you and yours. It's up to you to decide how much energy you need, and to ask for it. When you do, He will provide it.

Some days are light and breezy, but other days require quite a bit of heavy lifting. If the weight you're carrying seems a little too heavy, don't fret. God can provide the energy you need to carry your load. So what, Grandmother, are you waiting for?

*The power of God through His Spirit will work within us
to the degree that we permit it.*

Mrs. Charles E. Cowman

Adversity Builds Character

We also have joy with our troubles, because we know that these troubles produce patience. And patience produces character, and character produces hope.

Romans 5:3–4 NCV

The fact that we encounter adversity is not nearly so important as the way we choose to deal with it. And we must never forget that God intends for us to use our setbacks as stepping stones on the path to a better life.

When tough times arrive, we have a clear choice: we can begin the difficult work of tackling our troubles . . . or not. When we summon the courage to look Old Man Trouble squarely in the eye, he usually blinks. But if we refuse to address our problems, even the smallest annoyances have a way of growing into king-sized catastrophes.

We must build our lives on the Rock that cannot be shaken: we must trust in God. And then we must get on with the character-building, life-altering work of tackling our problems . . . because if we don't, who will? Or should?

Character cannot be developed in ease and quiet. Only through experience of trial and suffering can the soul be strengthened, vision cleared, ambition inspired, and success achieved.

Helen Keller

Keep Counting Your Blessings

I will bless them and the places surrounding my hill.
I will send down showers in season;
there will be showers of blessings.
Ezekiel 34:26 NIV

Have you counted your blessings lately? You should most certainly make thanksgiving a habit, a regular part of your daily routine. And while you're at it, you should encourage your children and grandchildren to do likewise. After all, when you pause to consider all the wonderful things that you and your loved ones have been given, isn't it right and proper to say thanks?

Today, take time to make a partial list of God's gifts to you: your family, your talents, your opportunities, your possessions, and the relationships you may, on occasion, take for granted. Then, when you've spent sufficient time listing your blessings, offer a prayer of gratitude to the Giver of all things good . . . and, to the best of your ability, make certain that you use your gifts wisely. Consider your life a thank-you note to God—and act accordingly.

Life does not have to be perfect to be wonderful.
Annette Funicello

Come Back to Him

Come back to the LORD and live!
Amos 5:6 NLT

Genuine repentance requires more than simply offering God apologies for our misdeeds. Real repentance may start with feelings of sorrow and remorse, but it ends only when we turn away from the sin that has heretofore distanced us from our Creator. In truth, we offer our most meaningful apologies to God, not with our words, but with our actions. As long as we are still engaged in sin, we may be "repenting," but we have not fully "repented."

Grandmother, is there an aspect of your life that is distancing you from your God? If so, ask for His forgiveness, and—just as important—correct your behavior. Then wrap yourself in the protection of God's promises. When you do, you will be secure.

When I prayerfully remember my shortcomings, I'm not
informing the Lord of anything he doesn't already know.
But when I enumerate my failings,
I take responsibility before him,
and he then releases me from dirty shame,
grimy guilt, and scummy sin.
Patsy Clairmont

September 17

Following Him Today

*Your old life is dead. Your new life, which is
your real life—even though invisible to spectators—
is with Christ in God. He is your life.*

Colossians 3:3 MSG

God's Word is clear: when we genuinely invite Him to reign over our hearts, and when we accept His transforming love, we are forever changed. When we welcome Christ into our hearts, an old life ends and a new way of living—along with a completely new way of viewing the world—begins.

Each morning offers a fresh opportunity to invite Jesus, yet once again, to guide our steps and to rule over our hearts and our days. Each morning presents yet another opportunity to take up His cross and follow in His footsteps. Today, let us rejoice in the new life that is ours through Christ, and let us follow Him, step by step, on the path that He first walked.

*God is not running an antique shop!
He is making all things new!*

Vance Havner

Will You Seek Him?

The LORD is with you when you are with Him.
If you seek Him, He will be found by you.

2 Chronicles 15:2 HCSB

If you are busy with more obligations than you have time to count, you know all too well that the demands of everyday life can, on occasion, seem overwhelming. Thankfully, even on the days when you feel overburdened, overworked, overstressed, and underappreciated, God is trying to get His message through . . . your job is to listen.

Are you discouraged, fearful, or just plain tired? If so, you can be comforted by the knowledge that God is with you. In whatever condition you find yourself—whether you are happy or sad, victorious or vanquished, troubled or triumphant—you can carve out moments of silent solitude to celebrate God's gifts and to experience His presence. When you do, you'll be reminded of an important truth: God is not just near, He is here. And He's ready to help you right here, right now.

Even when we cannot see the why and wherefore
of God's dealings, we know that there is love in
and behind them, so we can rejoice always.

J. I. Packer

Beyond the Distractions

Let's keep focused on that goal, those of us who want
everything God has for us. If any of you have something
else in mind, something less than total commitment,
God will clear your blurred vision—you'll see it yet!
Now that we're on the right track, let's stay on it.
Philippians 3:15–16 MSG

All of us must live through those days when the
traffic jams, the computer crashes, or the dog
makes a three-course meal out of the homework.
But when we find ourselves distracted by the minor
frustrations of life, we must catch ourselves, take a
deep breath, and lift our thoughts upward.

Sometimes, we must struggle mightily to rise
above the distractions of everyday living, but we need
never struggle alone. God is always with us—eternal
and faithful, with infinite patience and love—and if
we reach out to Him, He will restore our sense of
perspective and give peace to our souls.

So today, Grandmother, look above and beyond
all the distractions of twenty-first-century life, and
look to God. He never changes; He never waivers;
and He will never let you down.

There is an enormous power in little things
to distract our attention from God.
Oswald Chambers

When People Are Difficult

Judge not, and ye shall not be judged:
condemn not, and ye shall not be condemned:
forgive, and ye shall be forgiven.
Luke 6:37 KJV

As a woman who's seen her fair share of life, you know that people can be discourteous and cruel at times. Sometimes people can be unfair, unkind, and unappreciative. Sometimes folks get angry and frustrated. So what's a grandmother to do? God's answer is straightforward: forgive, forget, and move on.

Jesus was quick to forgive those who hurt Him, and you should do likewise. So today and every day make sure that you're quick to forgive others for their shortcomings. And when other people misbehave (as they most certainly will from time to time), don't pay too much attention. Just forgive those people as quickly as you can, and try to move on . . . as quickly as you can.

Judge your neighbor by his best moments,
not his worst.
Fulton J. Sheen

Choosing the Right Value System: God's

Choose my teachings instead of silver, and knowledge rather than the finest gold. Wisdom is more precious than rubies. Nothing you could want is equal to it.

Proverbs 8:10–11 NCV

Whether you realize it or not, your life is shaped by your values. And the same goes for your family members. From the time you wake in the morning until the moment you lay your head on the pillow at night, your actions are guided by the values that you hold most dear.

Society seeks to impose its set of values upon you and your loved ones; however, these values are often contrary to God's Word (and thus contrary to your best interests). The world's promises are incomplete and deceptive; God's promises are unfailing. Your challenge is to build your value system upon the firm foundation of God's promises. And while you're at it, Grandmother, please encourage your family members to do the same.

Having values keeps a person focused on the important things.

John Maxwell

Freedom from Those Pity Parties!

> [Jesus] did not many mighty works there
> because of their unbelief.
>
> Matthew 13:58 KJV

Have you ever invited yourself to a pity party? If so, you'll probably agree that you would have been much better off sending your regrets.

Self-pity is not only an unproductive way to think, it is also an affront to your Father in heaven. Self-pity and thanksgiving cannot coexist in the same mind. Bitterness and joy cannot coexist in the same heart. Gratitude and despair are mutually exclusive.

If your unreliable thoughts are allowing pain and worry to dominate your life, you must train yourself to think less about your troubles and more about God's blessings. When you stop to think about it, hasn't He given you enough blessings to occupy your thoughts all day, every day, from now on? Of course He has! So focus your mind on Him, and let your worries fend for themselves.

> *Self-pity is our worst enemy and if we yield to it,*
> *we can never do anything wise in the world.*
>
> Helen Keller

Arguments Lost

Refuse to get involved in inane discussions; they always end up in fights. God's servant must not be argumentative, but a gentle listener and a teacher who keeps cool, working firmly but patiently with those who refuse to obey.

2 Timothy 2:23–24 MSG

Arguments are seldom won but often lost. When we engage in petty squabbles, our losses usually outpace our gains. When we acquire the unfortunate habit of habitual bickering, we do harm to our spouses, to our friends, to our families, to our coworkers, and to ourselves.

Time and again, God's Word warns us that most arguments are a monumental waste of time, of energy, of life. In Titus, we are warned to refrain from "foolish arguments," and with good reason. Such arguments usually do more for the devil than they do for God.

So the next time you're tempted to engage in a silly squabble, whether inside the four walls of your home or outside them, refrain. When you do, you'll probably be doing everybody a favor, including yourself.

Argument is the worst sort of conversation.

Jonathan Swift

Changing the Status Quo

You were taught to leave your old self. . . . That old self becomes worse, because people are fooled by the evil things they want to do. But you were taught to be made new in your hearts, to become a new person. That new person is made to be like God—made to be truly good and holy.

Ephesians 4:22–24 NCV

If you're enduring tough times, it's easy to feel stuck. Easy, but wrong. With God, you're never really stuck anywhere for long because He is a God of infinite possibilities.

If you find yourself feeling as if you're mired in quicksand, stuck in a rut, or trapped in an unfortunate circumstance, abandon the status quo by making the changes that your heart tells you are right. After all, in God's glorious kingdom, there should be no place for women who are dejected, discouraged, or disheartened. God has a far better plan for you, Grandmother, and for your loved ones too. Your plan should be the same.

If God has you in the palm of his hand and your real life is secure in him, then you can venture forth—into the places and relationships, the challenges, the very heart of the storm— and you will be safe there.

Paula Rinehart

Too Comfortable?

Be not afraid, only believe.
Mark 5:36 KJV

Risk is an inevitable fact of life. From the moment we arise in the morning until the moment we drift off to sleep at night, we face a wide array of risks, both great and small.

Some risks, of course, should be avoided at all costs—these include risky behaviors that drive us further and further away from God's will for our lives. Yet other risks—the kinds of risks that we must take in order to expand our horizons and expand our faith—should be accepted as the inevitable price we must pay for living full and productive lives.

Okay, Grandmother, here's the big question: have you planted yourself firmly inside your own comfort zone? If so, it's time to reconsider the direction and scope of your activities. God has big plans for you, but those plans will most likely require you to expand your comfort zone—or leave it altogether.

With each new experience of letting God be in control, we gain courage and reinforcement for daring to do it again and again.
Gloria Gaither

And the Greatest of These

*Love is patient, love is kind and is not jealous;
love does not brag and is not arrogant, does not act
unbecomingly; it does not seek its own, is not provoked,
does not take into account a wrong suffered,
does not rejoice in unrighteousness, but rejoices
with the truth; bears all things, believes all things,
hopes all things, endures all things.*

1 Corinthians 13:4–7 NASB

The familiar words of 1 Corinthians 13 remind us of the importance of love. And love, like everything else in this wonderful world, begins and ends with God, but the middle part belongs to us. During the brief time that we have here on earth, God has given each of us the opportunity to become a loving person—or not. God has given each of us the opportunity to be kind, to be courteous, to be cooperative, and to be forgiving—or not. God has given each of us the chance to obey the Golden Rule, or to make up our own rules as we go. And God has created a world in which our choices have consequences. When we choose to love, to give, and to serve, we are blessed. It's as simple as that.

*You will find, as you look back upon your life,
that the moments when you have really lived
are the moments when you have done things
in the spirit of love.*

Henry Drummond

Pockets of Joy

I will thank you, Lord, with all my heart;
I will tell of all the marvelous things you have done.
I will be filled with joy because of you.
I will sing praises to your name, O Most High.

Psalm 9:1–2 NLT

Have you experienced real joy lately—the kind of joy that makes your heart soar? Hopefully so, because as a thoughtful, caring grandmother, you deserve it.

Should you expect to be a joy-filled woman twenty-four hours a day, seven days a week, from this moment on? No. But you can (and should) experience pockets of joy—moments when you are confronted by the immensity of God's gifts.

How can you find the kind of joy that lifts your heart and fills your soul? Start by consulting your heavenly Father every day. Then do all the good you can, wherever you can, whenever you can. Resolve to love everybody, starting with the people who are family. And spend a significant portion of every day thanking your Creator for His blessings. When you do these things, your joys will be multiplied and your life will be blessed.

God knows everything. He can manage everything, and
He loves us. Surely this is enough
for a fullness of joy that is beyond words.

Hannah Whitall Smith

Finding Silence

Be silent before the LORD and wait expectantly for Him.
Psalm 37:7 HCSB

The world seems to grow louder day by day, and our senses seem to be invaded at every turn. If we allow the distractions of a clamorous society to separate us from God's peace, we do ourselves a profound disservice. Our task, as dutiful believers, is to carve out moments of silence in a world filled with noise.

If we are to maintain righteous minds and compassionate hearts, we must take time each day for prayer and meditation. We must make ourselves still in the presence of our Creator. We must quiet our minds and our hearts so that we might sense God's will and His love.

Has the hectic pace of life robbed you, at least in part, of the joys of living? If so, Grandmother, it's time to reorder your priorities and your life. Nothing is more important than the time you spend with your heavenly Father. So be still and claim the genuine peace that is found in the silent moments you spend with God.

The world is full of noise. Might we not set ourselves to learn silence, stillness, solitude?
Elisabeth Elliot

He Is Close to the Brokenhearted

I am the Lord who heals you.

Exodus 15:26 NCV

When our friends or family members encounter life-shattering events, we struggle to find words that might offer them comfort and support. But finding the right words can be difficult, if not impossible. Sometimes, all that we can do is be with our loved ones and pray for them, trusting that God will do the rest.

Thankfully, God promises that He is "close to the brokenhearted" (Psalm 34:18 NIV). In times of intense sadness, we must turn to Him, and we must encourage our friends and family members to do likewise. When we do so, our Father comforts us and, in time, heals us.

Sometimes we need to be alone with our memories and our hurts. We just need to guard against making this our only response because it's not healthy. The Book of Psalms wants us to "cast your cares on the Lord and He will sustain you."

Billy Graham

The Simple Life

A pretentious, showy life is an empty life;
a plain and simple life is a full life.
Proverbs 13:7 MSG

You live in a world where simplicity is in short supply. Think for a moment about the complexity of your everyday life, and compare it to the lives of your ancestors. Certainly, you are the beneficiary of many technological innovations, but those innovations have a price: in all likelihood, your world is highly complex.

Unless you take firm control of your time and your life, you may be overwhelmed by an ever-increasing tidal wave of complexity that threatens your happiness. But your heavenly Father understands the joys of living simply, and so should you. So do yourself and your family a favor: keep your life as simple as possible. Simplicity is, indeed, genius. By simplifying your life, you are destined to improve it.

I am beginning to learn that it is the sweet,
simple things of life which are
the real ones after all.
Laura Ingalls Wilder

October

Thank-You Hug for Grandmother

Dear Grandmother,

Thanks for your patience. The rigors of caring for a family can test the patience of the most even-tempered woman, and you were more patient than most.

All of us, grandparents and kids alike, make our share of mistakes. When we made our own mistakes, you dried our tears, you forgave us, and you convinced us that we could recover. We thank God for your patience, for your faith, and for your love.

The Chains of Perfectionism

If you wait for perfect conditions,
you will never get anything done.
Ecclesiastes 11:4 NLT

Hey, Grandmother, here's an important question: are you bound up by the chains of perfectionism? If so, it's time to do the wise thing; it's time to lighten up on yourself and your family.

Of course you and your loved ones should work hard; of course you, and they, should be disciplined; of course you should do your best. But then, when you and yours have done your best, you should be satisfied with the results.

In heaven, we will know perfection. Here on earth, we have a few short years to wrestle with the challenges of imperfection. Let us accept these lives that God has given us—with open, loving arms.

How important it is that we give up
our expectations of perfection
in any area of our lives.
Fred Rogers

Teaching Lessons About Self-Respect

*You made all the delicate, inner parts of my body
and knit me together in my mother's womb.
Thank you for making me so wonderfully complex!
Your workmanship is marvelous—and how well I know it.*
Psalm 139:13–14 NLT

When your children and grandchildren look in the mirror, are they staring back at their biggest boosters or their harshest critics? And what are you teaching your clan about the importance of self-image? If you can help your kids and grandkids learn to give themselves the benefit of the doubt—if you can teach them how to have constructive conversations with the person they see on their photo IDs—you will have given them a wonderful gift.

Your loved ones inhabit a world in which self-respect is often in short supply. So it's important for kids (of all ages) to acquire the habit of thinking constructively about themselves, their circumstances, and their opportunities. When they do, they can avoid the mental quicksand of continual self-criticism, and they can get about the business of celebrating this grand opportunity called life. You can help them sort all this out, Grandmother. And the time to help them sort it out is now.

*He who is able to love himself
is able to love others also.*
Paul Tillich

Finding Happiness and Abundance

*Happy are those who fear the L*ORD*.*
Yes, happy are those who delight in doing
what he commands.
Psalm 112:1 NLT

Do you seek happiness, abundance, and contentment? If so, here are some things you should do: love God and depend upon Him for strength; try, to the best of your abilities, to follow God's plan for your life; and strive to follow in the footsteps of His Son. When you do these things, you'll discover that happiness goes hand in hand with godliness.

What does life have in store for you and your loved ones? A world full of possibilities (of course it's up to you to seize them) and God's promise of abundance (of course it's up to you to accept it). So, Grandmother, as you embark upon the next phase of your life's journey, remember to celebrate the life that God has given you. Your Creator has blessed you beyond measure. Honor Him with your prayers, your words, your deeds, and your joy.

Make God's will the focus of your life day by day.
If you seek to please Him and Him alone,
you'll find yourself satisfied with life.
Kay Arthur

Ask and Obey

Ask in my name, according to my will,
and he'll most certainly give it to you.
Your joy will be a river overflowing its banks!
John 16:24 MSG

God gives the gifts; we, as God's children, should accept them—but oftentimes, we don't. Why? Because we fail to trust our heavenly Father completely and because we are, at times, surprisingly stubborn.

Stubbornness is a naturally occurring human trait that infects even the most well meaning among us, almost from birth. We want to do things in our own way and in our own time, even if it means disregarding God's wisdom.

Okay, Grandmother, please be honest: have you been guilty of doing things your way instead of God's way? If so, you're missing out on some of the Creator's richest blessings. So here's a hint: whenever you have an important choice to make, consult your Father in heaven, and heed His advice. Then get ready for God to shower you with more blessings than you can count, because that's precisely what He has promised to do.

Faithfulness today is the best preparation
for the demands of tomorrow.
Elisabeth Elliot

Purpose and Service

*Your attitude should be the same as that of
Christ Jesus. . . . Taking the very nature of a servant . . .*
Philippians 2:5, 7 NIV

As you seek to discover God's purpose for your life, you may rest assured that His plan for you is centered on service—service to your family, your friends, your church, your community, and the world.

And it's not just enough to be a servant; you must also strive to be a humble servant. When you learn to serve others with genuine humility in your heart, you will glorify yourself not before men, but before God, and that's what God intends. After all, earthly glory is fleeting: here today and soon gone. But heavenly glory endures throughout eternity.

So the choice is yours, Grandmom: either you can lift yourself up here on earth and be humbled in heaven, or vice versa. Choose vice versa.

*God never calls without enabling us.
In other words, if he calls you to do something,
he makes it possible for you to do it.*
Luci Swindoll

No Shortcuts

We must do the works of Him
who sent Me while it is day.
Night is coming when no one can work.

John 9:4 HCSB

Wise grandparents (like you) teach their grand-children the importance of discipline, using both words and examples, with a decided emphasis on the latter. After all, life's greatest rewards seldom fall into our laps; to the contrary, our greatest accomplishments usually require lots of work, which is perfectly fine with God. After all, He knows that we're up to the task.

The world often conspires to teach our kids that it's perfectly okay to look for shortcuts. But as concerned adults, we must teach our children that success is earned by working hard, not by getting by. When we teach our kids to work diligently and consistently, they can expect to earn rich rewards for their efforts. But our youngsters must never expect their rewards to precede their labors.

There are no shortcuts to any place worth going.

Beverly Sills

Real Prosperity

*Serving God does make us very rich, if we are satisfied
with what we have. We brought nothing into the world,
so we can take nothing out. But, if we have food and
clothes, we will be satisfied with that.*
1 Timothy 6:6–8 NCV

We live in an era of prosperity, a time when
many of us have been richly blessed with an
assortment of material possessions that our forebears
could have scarcely imagined. As grandparents living
in these prosperous times, we must be cautious, and
we must keep prosperity in perspective.

The world stresses the importance of material
possessions; God does not. The world offers the
promise of happiness through wealth and public
acclaim; God offers the promise of peace through
His Son. When in doubt, we must distrust the world
and trust God. The world often makes promises that
it cannot keep, but when God makes a promise, He
keeps it not just for a day or a year or a lifetime but
for all eternity.

*It's sobering to contemplate how much time, effort,
sacrifice, compromise, and attention we give to acquiring
and increasing our supply of something that is totally
insignificant in eternity.*
Anne Graham Lotz

October 8

Living and Laughing

Laugh with your happy friends when they're happy.
Romans 12:15 MSG

Every relationship, whether it is with your spouse, your kids, your grandkids, or your coworkers, can (and should) be seasoned with good, clean fun. But sometimes, instead of viewing our world with a mixture of optimism and humor, we allow worries and distractions to rob us of the joy that God intends for our lives.

If you're suffering from the inevitable demands of twenty-first-century parenting, you know all too well that a good laugh can seem hard to find. But it need not be so. And if you're having trouble getting your funny bone in gear, here's a helpful hint: lighten up and don't take things so seriously (especially yourself). When you do, you'll soon learn that everything goes better when you learn to laugh more and fret less.

Your life is either a comedy or a drama, depending upon how you look at it. Make yours a comedy.

If you want people to feel comfortable around you, to enjoy being with you, then learn to laugh at yourself and find humor in life's little mishaps.
Dennis Swanberg

You're on a Mission

*Everything, absolutely everything, above and below,
visible and invisible, rank after rank after rank
of angels—everything got started in him
and finds its purpose in him.*

Colossians 1:16 MSG

Whether you realize it or not, Grandmother, you are on a personal mission for God. As a parent and grandparent, that mission is straightforward: honor God, guide your family, and serve those in need.

Some days the challenges of everyday life may seem overwhelming, but you should never become discouraged. You and God, working together, can handle anything that comes your way—and the more demanding your job becomes, the more you need to avail yourself of God's power and His peace.

Every day offers countless opportunities to serve God while serving your loved ones. When you do so, your Creator will bless you in miraculous ways. That's why you should always place God where He belongs: at the very center of your family and your life.

We are all pencils in the hand of God.

Mother Teresa

When It's Time to Decide

God has not given us a spirit of fearfulness,
but one of power, love, and sound judgment.
2 Timothy 1:7 HCSB

Sometimes we face problems that defy easy solutions. If you find yourself facing a difficult decision, here's a simple formula for making the right choice: let God decide. Instead of fretting about your future, pray about it.

When you consult your heavenly Father early and often, you'll soon discover that the quiet moments you spend with God can be very helpful. Many times, God will quietly lead you along a path of His choosing, a path that is right for you.

So, Grandmother, the next time you arrive at one of life's inevitable crossroads, take a moment or two to bow your head and have a chat with the Ultimate Advisor. When you do, you'll never stay lost for long.

When we learn to listen to Christ's voice
for the details of our daily decisions,
we begin to know Him personally.
Catherine Marshall

Time: A Nonrenewable Resource

*While it is daytime, we must continue doing
the work of the One who sent me.
Night is coming, when no one can work.*
John 9:4 NCV

As you've certainly learned by now, there simply isn't enough time to do everything you want—or, for that matter, need—to do. That's why you must be very careful about the way you choose to spend the time that God has given you.

Time is a nonrenewable gift from the Creator. But sometimes we treat our time here on earth as if it were not a gift at all. We may be tempted to invest our lives in petty diversions or in trivial pursuits. But our Father in heaven beckons each of us to a higher calling.

Each waking moment holds the potential for you to do a good deed, to say a kind word, or to offer a heartfelt prayer. Each day is a special treasure to be savored and celebrated. Every heartbeat marks yet another opportunity to do the right thing and to give thanks to the proper Source. And because time is short, the best time to give thanks is now.

*Time is so precious that God deals it out
only second by second.*
Fulton J. Sheen

Beyond Jealousy

*Where jealousy and selfishness are,
there will be confusion and every kind of evil.*
James 3:14 NCV

Are you too wise to be consumed with feelings of jealousy? Hopefully so. After all, the Bible clearly teaches us to love our neighbors, not to envy them. But sometimes, despite our best intentions, we fall prey to feelings of resentfulness, jealousy, bitterness, and envy. Why? Because we are human, and because we live in a world that places great importance on material possessions (possessions that, by the way, are totally unimportant to God).

So the next time you feel pangs of envy invading your thoughts, remind yourself of two things: (1) envy is wrong, and (2) God has already showered you with so many blessings (starting with your family) that as a thoughtful, thankful grandmother, you have no right to be envious of any other person on earth.

*Never indulge in jealousy or envy.
Those two destructive emotions will eat you alive.*
Loretta Young

God's Faithfulness

Because of the LORD's faithful love we do not perish,
for His mercies never end.
They are new every morning; great is Your faithfulness!
Lamentations 3:22–23 HCSB

God is faithful to us even when we are not very faithful to Him. God keeps His promises to us even when we stray far from His path. God offers us countless blessings, blessings that, by the way, we don't always accept. If we are to experience His love and His grace, we must claim these rewards for ourselves.

God is with you right now, so listen prayerfully to the quiet voice of your heavenly Father. Talk with Him often; seek His guidance; watch for His signs; listen to the wisdom that He shares through the reliable voice of your own conscience. And remember, Grandmother, that God loves you, and He loves your family. He has gifts He wants to share with you. Accept those gifts today.

We are of such value to God that He came to live among
us . . . and to guide us home. He will go to any length to
seek us, even to being lifted high
upon the cross to draw us back to Himself.
We can only respond by loving God for His love.
Catherine of Siena

October 14

Strength for Your Daily Journey

> God is our refuge and strength,
> a very present help in trouble.
>
> Psalm 46:1 NKJV

Even the most inspired grandmothers can, from time to time, find themselves running on empty. Why? Because the inevitable demands of daily life can be very draining, that's why!

Are you almost too weary to lift your head? Then bow it—in prayer. Are you almost too tired to spend another moment on your feet? Then get on your knees. If you ask God to strengthen you—if you petition Him with a sincere and obedient heart—He will give you the power and the courage to meet any challenge.

Your search to discover God's purpose for your life is not a destination; it is a journey that unfolds day by day. And that's exactly how often you should seek direction and strength from your Creator: one day at a time, each day followed by the next, without exception.

> When I feel afraid, and think I've lost my way,
> still You're right there beside me.
> Nothing will I fear as long as You are near.
>
> Amy Grant

Drawing Courage from God

That is why we can say with confidence,
"The Lord is my helper, so I will not be afraid.
What can mere mortals do to me?"

Hebrews 13:6 NLT

Life can be difficult and discouraging at times. During our darkest moments, we can depend upon our friends and family, and upon God. When we do, we find the courage to face even the darkest days with hopeful hearts and willing hands.

Are you ready to do as God asks and lay all your pain, desires, fears, and hopes on Him? If so, then you will discover a newfound strength, compliments of God.

So when you find yourself worried about the challenges of today or the uncertainties of tomorrow, you must ask yourself whether or not you are ready to place your concerns and your life in God's all-powerful, all-knowing, all-loving hands. If the answer to that question is yes—as it should be—then you can draw courage today from the source of strength that never fails: your heavenly Father.

God knows that the strength that comes from wrestling
with our fear will give us wings to fly.

Paula Rinehart

Faith That Works

*The righteousness of God is revealed from faith to faith;
as it is written, "The just shall live by faith."*

Romans 1:17 NKJV

Through every stage of your life, God stands by your side, ready to strengthen you and protect you . . . if you have faith in Him. When you place your faith, your trust, indeed your life in the hands of Christ Jesus, you'll be amazed at the marvelous things He can do with you and through you.

So make this promise to yourself and keep it: make certain that your faith is a faith that works. How? You can strengthen your faith through praise, through worship, through Bible study, and through prayer. When you do so, you'll learn to trust God's plans. With Him, all things are possible, and He stands ready to open a world of possibilities to you . . . if you have faith.

*Faith is obedience at home and looking
to the Master; obedience is faith
going out to do His will.*

Andrew Murray

Meeting the Obligations

*In all the work you are doing, work the best you can.
Work as if you were doing it for the Lord, not for people.*

Colossians 3:23 NCV

N obody needs to tell you the obvious: you have lots of responsibilities—obligations to yourself, to your family, to your community, and to your God. And which of these duties should take priority? The answer can be found in Matthew 6:33: "Seek first the kingdom of God and His righteousness, and all these things will be provided for you" (HCSB).

When you "seek first the kingdom of God," all your other obligations have a way of falling into place. When you honor God with your time, your talents. and your prayers, you'll be much more likely to count your blessings instead of your troubles.

So do yourself and your loved ones a favor: take all your duties seriously, especially your duties to God. When you do, you'll discover that pleasing your Father in heaven isn't just the right thing to do; it's also the best way to live.

*In the very place where God has put us,
whatever its limitations, whatever kind of work it may be,
we may indeed serve the Lord Christ.*

Elisabeth Elliot

Full Confidence

May the God of hope fill you with all joy and peace as
you trust in him, so that you may overflow with hope
by the power of the Holy Spirit.

Romans 15:13 NIV

A re you a confident grandmother, or do you live under a cloud of uncertainty and doubt? The answer to this question will determine, in large part, how you view your family, your future, your work, and your world. As the saying goes, "Attitude determines altitude." The higher your hopes, the higher you're likely to soar.

Yet even the most confident will encounter situations that raise doubts and fears. You are no exception. But when you see those inevitable storm clouds on the horizon, don't ever lose hope. After all, you're part of a loving family, you possess unique talents, you have the determination and the courage to tackle your problems, and you are always in the presence of the Ultimate Partner. With God and family by your side, you have every reason to be confident . . . very confident.

As I have grown in faith and confidence,
I have known more and more that my worth is based on
the love of God.

Leslie Williams

Being Wary of Society's Priorities

Do not love the world or the things in the world.
If anyone loves the world,
the love of the Father is not in him.

1 John 2:15 NKJV

The world makes promises that it simply cannot fulfill. It promises happiness, contentment, prosperity, and abundance. But genuine, lasting abundance is not a function of worldly possessions; it is a function of our thoughts, our actions, and the relationship we choose to create with our God. The world's promises are incomplete and illusory; God's promises are unfailing. We must build our lives on the firm foundation of God's promises . . . nothing else will suffice.

Society's priorities are transitory; God's priorities are permanent. The world's treasures are difficult to find and difficult to keep; God's treasures are ever-present and everlasting. Which treasures and whose priorities will you claim as your own? The answer should be obvious.

Aim at heaven and you will get earth thrown in;
aim at earth and you will get neither.

C. S. Lewis

When a Grandmother Speaks . . .

A good person produces good deeds and words
season after season.
Matthew 12:35 MSG

When a grandmother speaks, her family notices. In fact, a grandma's words and how she chooses to say them, can set the emotional tone for her entire family. When a grandmother is respectful, enthusiastic, and kind, her children and grandchildren are continually blessed by the good words and good deeds of the woman they love.

God intends that we speak words of kindness, wisdom, and truth. When we do, we share a priceless gift with our family members. So today, Grandmother, be sure to choose your words carefully. Be encouraging; be hopeful; be truthful; be kind. And remember that your loved ones don't just need advice, they also need a positive role model, a woman they can trust and admire. A woman like you.

I shall pass through life but once.
Let me show kindness now,
as I shall not pass this way again.
William Penn

Choosing to Be Kind

Kind people do themselves a favor,
but cruel people bring trouble on themselves.
Proverbs 11:17 NCV

Kindness is a choice. Sometimes, when we feel happy or prosperous, we find it easy to be kind. Other times, when we are discouraged or tired, we can scarcely summon the energy to utter a single kind word. But, God's commandment is clear: we must observe the Golden Rule "in everything." God intends that we make the conscious choice to treat others with kindness and respect, no matter our circumstances, no matter our emotions. Kindness, therefore, is a choice that we must make many times each day.

When we weave the thread of kindness into the very fabric of our lives, we enrich our own lives by enriching the lives of others. And everybody is better for it.

Reach out and care for someone who needs
the touch of hospitality. The time you spend caring today
will be a love gift that will blossom into
the fresh joy of God's Spirit in the future.
Emilie Barnes

Eternal Wisdom

*Happy is the person who finds wisdom
and gains understanding.*
Proverbs 3:13 NLT

Sometimes, amid the concerns of everyday life, we lose perspective. Life seems out of balance as we confront an array of demands that sap our strength and cloud our thoughts. What's needed is a renewed faith, a fresh perspective, and God's wisdom.

Here in the twenty-first century, commentary is commonplace and information is everywhere. But the ultimate source of wisdom, the kind of timeless wisdom that God willingly shares with His children, is still available from a unique source: the Holy Bible.

The wisdom of the world changes with the ever-shifting sands of public opinion. God's wisdom does not. His wisdom is eternal. It never changes. And it most certainly is the wisdom that you, as an insightful woman and a thoughtful grandparent, should use to plan your day and your life.

*Wisdom always waits for the right time to act,
while emotion always pushes for action right now.*
Joyce Meyer

Everyday Crises

*We take the good days from God—
why not also the bad days?*
Job 2:10 MSG

You live in a world that seeks to snare your attention and lead you away from God. Each time you are tempted to distance yourself from the Creator, you will face a spiritual crisis. A few of these crises may be monumental in scope, but most will be the small, everyday decisions of life. In fact, life here on earth can be seen as one test after another—and with each crisis comes yet another opportunity to grow closer to God . . . or to distance yourself from His plan for your life.

Today, you will face many opportunities to say yes to your Creator—and you will also encounter many opportunities to say no to Him. Your answers will determine the quality of your day and the direction of your life, so answer carefully . . . very carefully.

*Crisis brings us face to face with our inadequacy
and our inadequacy in turn leads us to
the inexhaustible sufficiency of God.*
Catherine Marshall

Seeking His Will

Teach me to do Your will, for You are my God;
Your Spirit is good. Lead me in the land of uprightness.
Psalm 143:10 NKJV

The book of Judges tells the story of Deborah, the fearless woman who helped lead the army of Israel to victory over the Canaanites. Deborah was a judge and a prophetess, a woman called by God to lead her people. And when she answered God's call, she was rewarded with one of the great victories of Old Testament times.

Like Deborah, all of us are called to serve our Creator. And, like Deborah, we may sometimes find ourselves facing trials that can bring trembling to the very depths of our souls. What should we do? We, like Deborah, should entrust our lives to God completely and without reservation. When we do, He gives us courage for today, hope for tomorrow, and joy for all eternity.

The only safe place is in the center of God's will. It is not
only the safest place. It is also the most rewarding and the
most satisfying place to be.
Gigi Graham Tchividjian

Sharing Your Joy

Every day is hard for those who suffer,
but a happy heart is like a continual feast.
Proverbs 15:15 NCV

Are you a grandmother whose joy is evident for all to see? Do you spread the seeds of good cheer and celebration wherever you go? If so, congratulations: your joyful spirit serves as a powerful example to your family and friends. And because of your attitude, you may be assured that your family will heed the words of Proverbs 31:28 (NASB) as they "rise up" and call you blessed.

God's plan for you and your clan includes family-sized helpings of abundance and joy. Claim these gifts today. And as you do so, remind yourself and your loved ones that God continuously offers more blessings than any of you can count. He offers His abundance, He offers His peace, and He offers His joy. You must accept these gifts and share them freely, starting today and ending never.

A joyful heart is the inevitable result
of a heart burning with love.
Mother Teresa

Trust Yourself

*They show that in their hearts they know
what is right and wrong.*
Romans 2:15 NCV

Hey, Grandmother, are you willing to trust your instincts? Hopefully so. After all, God gave you intuition for a very good reason: to use it. But sometimes, especially in times of crisis, it's hard to trust your own instincts because your inner voice—the conscience that resides within you and the intuition that seeks to guide you—can be drowned out by fear, worry, anxiety, or confusion. That's why during times of crisis, you must do whatever it takes to look deep within your own heart.

If you're facing a difficult question or an important decision, your most trusted advisor may very well be that quiet voice within. So when your inner voice starts talking, take careful mental notes. And when in doubt, trust yourself.

*There is a balance to be maintained in situations.
That balance is the Holy Spirit within us to guide us into
the truth of each situation and circumstance
in which we find ourselves. He will provide us
the wisdom to know when we are to be adaptable
and adjustable and when we are to take
a firm stand and be immovable.*
Joyce Meyer

October 27

Managing Your Talents and Treasures

Do not neglect the gift that is in you.
1 Timothy 4:14 NKJV

Your talents, resources, and opportunities are all gifts from the Giver of all things good. And the best way to express your gratitude for His gifts is to use them.

Do you have a particular talent? Hone your skill and use it. Do you possess financial resources? Share them. Have you been blessed by a particular opportunity, or have you experienced unusual good fortune? Use your good fortune to help others.

When you share the gifts God has given you—and when you share them freely and without fanfare—you invite God to bless you more and more. So today, Grandmother, please do yourself and the world a favor: be a faithful manager of your talents and treasures. And then prepare yourself for even greater blessings that are sure to come.

I would strongly recommend to you to improve your talents; let not one lie buried in the earth.
Maria W. Stewart

Becoming Unstuck

*Grow in grace and understanding of our Master
and Savior, Jesus Christ.
Glory to the Master, now and forever! Yes!*
2 Peter 3:18 MSG

Bitterness is a roadblock on the path that God has planned for your life. If you allow yourself to become resentful, discouraged, envious, or embittered, you will become spiritually stuck. But if you obey God's Word and forgive those who have harmed you, you will experience God's peace as you follow His path.

The Bible teaches us that forgiveness is never optional; forgiveness is required of those who seek to follow God's path and trust His instruction.

You are a woman who has much to share with your family and your world. And God intends to use you in wonderful, unexpected ways if you let Him. The decision to seek God's plan and to follow it is yours and yours alone. Please don't let bitterness get in the way.

*Better by far you should forget and smile
than you should remember and be sad.*
Christina Rossetti

Infinite Possibilities

*We know that all things work together for the good
of those who love God: those who are called
according to His purpose.*

Romans 8:28 HCSB

Ours is a God of infinite possibilities. But sometimes, because of limited vision and limited understanding, we wrongly assume that God cannot or will not intervene in the affairs of mankind. Such assumptions are simply wrong.

Are you afraid to ask God to do big things in your life? Is your faith a little threadbare or perhaps a little worn? If so, it's time to abandon your doubts and reclaim your faith in God's promises.

God's Word makes it clear: absolutely nothing is impossible for Him. And since the Bible means what it says, you can be comforted in the knowledge that the Creator of the universe can do miraculous things in your own life and in the lives of your loved ones. Your challenge is to take God at His word and expect the miraculous. When you do your part, He will most assuredly do His.

The impossible is exactly what God does.

Oswald Chambers

How Important Is Money?

*The love of money is a root of all kinds of evil,
and by craving it, some have wandered away from
the faith and pierced themselves with many pains.*
1 Timothy 6:10 HCSB

Our society holds material possessions in high
regard . . . very high regard. Far too many people
seem to worship money and the things that money
can buy, but such misplaced priorities inevitably
lead to disappointments and dissatisfaction. Popular
opinion to the contrary, money cannot buy happiness,
period.

Money, in and of itself, is not evil; but the worship
of money inevitably leads to troublesome behavior.

When we worship God, we are blessed. But if
we dare to worship the almighty dollar, we invite
headaches and heartaches. So today, Grandmother,
as you prioritize matters of importance for you and
yours, remember that God is almighty, but the dollar
is not.

*Have you prayed about your resources lately?
Find out how God wants you to use your time
and your money. No matter what it costs,
forsake all that is not of God.*
Kay Arthur

It Pays to Praise

Through Jesus let us always offer to God our sacrifice
of praise, coming from lips that speak his name.
Hebrews 13:15 NCV

The Bible makes it clear: it pays to praise God. But sometimes we allow ourselves to become so preoccupied with the demands of everyday life that we forget to say thank you to the Giver of all good gifts.

Worship and praise should be a part of everything we do. Otherwise, we quickly lose perspective as we fall prey to the demands of the moment.

Do you sincerely desire to be a worthy servant of the One who has given you a loving family, eternal love, and eternal life? Of course you do! So praise Him for who He is and for what He has done for you and yours. And one more thing: don't just praise Him on Sunday morning, Grandmother. Praise Him all day long, every day, for as long as you live . . . and then for all eternity.

Two wings are necessary to lift our souls
toward God: prayer and praise.
Prayer asks. Praise accepts the answer.
Mrs. Charles E. Cowman

November

Thank-You Hug for Grandmother

Dear Grandmother,

You always seemed to understand that a grandparent's attitude is contagious. Thanks for your positive attitude. When we found ourselves dwelling on the negatives of life, you helped us count our blessings instead of our troubles. Your optimism is contagious—it gives us the courage to dream . . . and the faith to believe that our dreams can come true.

He's Ready . . . Are You?

*Watch therefore, and pray always
that you may be counted worthy.*
Luke 21:36 NKJV

Jesus made it clear to His disciples: they should pray always. And so should we. Genuine, heartfelt prayer changes things and it changes us. When we lift our hearts to our Father in heaven, we open ourselves to a never-ending source of divine wisdom and infinite love.

Do you have questions that you simply can't answer? Ask for the guidance of your Creator. Whatever your need, no matter how great or small, pray about it. When you do, you can be certain that God hears your prayers.

God is not just near; He is right here watching after you and your loved ones. His hand is reshaping your family, your community, and your world. He is always ready to talk with you. Are you ready to talk to Him?

*Cultivating a heart of prayer is a sure way to experience
God's presence.*
Elizabeth George

November 2

Your Beliefs and You

The kingdom of God is not in talk but in power.
1 Corinthians 4:20 HCSB

Our theology must be demonstrated, not by our words, but by our actions. So we must do our best to make certain that our actions are accurate reflections of our beliefs. We may proclaim our beliefs to our hearts' content, but our proclamations will mean nothing—to our children, to our grandchildren or to ourselves—unless we accompany our words with deeds that match.

The sermons we live are far more compelling than the ones we give. So remember, Grandmother, whether you like it or not, your life is an accurate reflection of your creed. And your loved ones are always watching. If this fact gives you cause for concern, don't hesitate to give yourself a pep talk. And then when your good deeds speak for themselves—as they most certainly will—don't interrupt.

What you do reveals what you believe about God,
regardless of what you say. When God reveals what He
has purposed to do, you face a crisis—
a decision time. God and the world can tell from your
response what you really believe about God.
Henry Blackaby

God's Perspective . . . and Yours

Since you have been raised to new life with Christ,
set your sights on the realities of heaven, where Christ sits
at God's right hand in the place of honor and power.
Colossians 3:1 NLT

Even if you're the world's most thoughtful grandmother, you may, from time to time, lose perspective—it happens on those days when life seems out of balance and pressures seem overwhelming. What's needed is a fresh perspective, a restored sense of balance . . . and God.

If a temporary loss of perspective has left you worried, exhausted, or both, it's time to readjust your thought patterns. Negative thoughts are habit forming; thankfully, so are positive ones. With practice, you can form the habit of focusing on God's priorities and your possibilities. When you do, you'll spend less time fretting about your challenges and more time praising God for His gifts.

So, Grandmother, pray for a sense of balance and perspective. And remember, your thoughts are intensely powerful, so handle them with care.

The proper perspective creates within us
a spirit of reaching outside of ourselves with
joy and enthusiasm.
Luci Swindoll

Choices

*I am offering you life or death, blessings or curses.
Now, choose life! . . . To choose life is to love the LORD
your God, obey him, and stay close to him.*

Deuteronomy 30:19–20 NCV

As a savvy grandmom, you know that the quality
of your life depends, to a surprising extent, on
the quality of the choices you make. And the same
goes for the rest of your clan. So if you and yours
desire to experience lives of abundance and significance, you must make choices that are pleasing to the
Creator.

From the instant you wake up in the morning
until the moment you nod off to sleep at night, you
make lots of decisions: decisions about the things
you do, decisions about the words you speak, and
decisions about the thoughts you choose to think.

Today, remember that wise choices are rewarded,
while unwise ones are not. So make the kinds of
choices that enhance your relationship with God.
After all, He deserves no less than your best . . . and
so, for that matter, do you.

*Every day of our lives we make choices
about how we're going to live that day.*
Luci Swindoll

Help Your Family Keep Growing

*Dear brothers and sisters, whenever trouble comes
your way, let it be an opportunity for joy. For when your
faith is tested, your endurance has a chance to grow.
So let it grow, for when your endurance is fully developed,
you will be strong in character and ready for anything.*

James 1:2–4 NLT

As a grandmother, you have a profound respon
sibility to be a positive role model to your family. So here's a question that should make you pause
and think: do you want your family to keep growing
intellectually, emotionally, and spiritually? If you
answered yes (which, undoubtedly, you did), you've
simply got to keep growing too. As a responsible role
model, you must continue to expand your horizons
through every stage of life.

Growth is sometimes painful; it's sometimes
earned at a very high price; but for thoughtful women
(like you) personal growth is always worth the cost.

Today you will encounter circumstances, perhaps
troubling circumstances, that will offer you opportunities to grow or not. Choose growth—it's the highest
and best way to live.

The secret of a happy life: Accept change gracefully.

Jimmy Stewart

Today Is a Gift

The LORD is king! Let the earth rejoice!
Let the farthest islands be glad.
Psalm 97:1 NLT

This day is a gift from God. How will you use it? Will you celebrate God's gifts and share words of encouragement and hope with all who cross your path? Will you trust in the Father and praise His glorious handiwork? The answer to these questions will determine, to a surprising extent, the quality, the direction, and the tone of your day.

For thoughtful grandmoms (like you), every new day is a cause for robust celebration. So today give thanks for the gift of life and for the One who created it. And give life to your loved ones, that little clan that gives meaning to your life. Then use this day—a day that is another wonderful gift from the Father above—to serve your Creator, your family, and your community.

Live today fully, expressing gratitude
for all you have been, all you are right now,
and all you are becoming.
Melodie Beattie

When Faith Begins to Slip Away

*Immediately the father of the child cried out
and said with tears, "Lord, I believe; help my unbelief!"*
Mark 9:24 NKJV

Doubts come in several shapes and sizes: doubts about God, doubts about the future, and doubts about our own abilities, for starters. But when doubts creep in, as they will from time to time, we need not despair. As Sheila Walsh observed, "To wrestle with God does not mean that we have lost faith, but that we are fighting for it."

God never leaves our side, not for an instant. He is always with us, always willing to calm the storms of life. When we sincerely seek His presence—and when we genuinely seek to establish a deeper, more meaningful relationship with Him—God is prepared to touch our hearts, to calm our fears, to answer our doubts, and to restore our confidence.

*We are most vulnerable to the piercing winds of doubt
when we distance ourselves from the mission and
fellowship to which Christ has called us.*
Joni Eareckson Tada

Sharing Words of Encouragement

Good people's words will help many others.

Proverbs 10:21 NCV

The words that we speak have the power to do great good or great harm. If we speak words of encouragement and hope, we can lift others up. And that's exactly what God instructs us to do.

Even a small act of kindness can make a big difference in someone's life. So how many people will you encourage today? Five? Ten? Twenty? Even more than that? The answer you give will help determine the quality of *their* lives and the quality of *your* life, so answer carefully.

When you share the gift of encouragement, you share a priceless gift with your family and the world. The time to share that gift is most certainly now. You can never speak a kind word too soon or too often.

In all your deeds and words, you should
look on Jesus as your model,
whether you are keeping silence or speaking, whether you
are alone or with others.

St. Bonaventure

Teaching the Importance of Character

People with integrity have firm footing,
but those who follow crooked paths will slip and fall.
Proverbs 10:9 NLT

Wise grandmothers teach the importance of character. Character doesn't spring up overnight; it grows gradually over a lifetime. It is the sum of every right decision, every honest word, every noble thought, and every heartfelt prayer. Character is a precious thing—difficult to build, but easy to tear down; wise grandmothers value it and protect it at all costs . . . and they encourage their children and grandchildren to do the same.

Are you serious about teaching your family the importance of integrity, through your words and your deeds? Of course you are . . . and so, for that matter, is God. So here's the challenge: consider God to be your partner as you teach family and friends. And then, with no further delay, let the character building begin . . . today.

Often, our character is at greater risk in
prosperity than in adversity.
Beth Moore

The Rule That's Golden

This royal law is found in the Scriptures:
"Love your neighbor as you love yourself."
If you obey this law, then you are doing right.
James 2:8 ICB

Is the Golden Rule one of the rules that governs your household? Hopefully so. Obeying the Golden Rule is a proven way to improve all your relationships, including your relationships with the people who happen to live inside the four walls of your home. But the reverse is also true: if you or your loved ones ignore the Golden Rule, you're headed for trouble, and fast.

God's Word makes it clear: we are to treat our loved ones with respect, kindness, fairness, and courtesy. And He knows we can do so if we try. So, Grandmother, if you're wondering how you should treat your loved ones—or anybody else, for that matter—just ask the woman you see every time you look in the mirror. The answer you receive will tell you exactly what to do.

Be so preoccupied with good will
that you haven't room for ill will.
E. Stanley Jones

Cleaning Up the Mental Mess

*Fix your thoughts on what is true and honorable
and right. Think about things that are pure and lovely
and admirable. Think about things that are
excellent and worthy of praise.*

Philippians 4:8 NLT

Mental garbage has a way of gradually building up in the minds of even the most optimistic grandparents, so you should keep yourself on guard against that messy collection of negative thoughts, wrongheaded ideas, irrational notions, and unhelpful ruminations that can, at times, swirl around in your brain. Those kinds of thoughts have the power to turn your mind into the psychological equivalent of a landfill.

When you feel that your healthy thoughts have morphed into sloppy thinking, it's time to take out the garbage by talking to someone you can trust and by talking to God. When you do, you'll start recycling those bad thoughts and turning them into good ones.

So the next time your thoughts migrate toward the negative end of the spectrum, do the healthy thing: open up your mind . . . and take out the trash.

*Optimism is that faith that leads to achievement. Nothing
can be done without hope and confidence.*

Helen Keller

Beyond Blame

Get rid of all bitterness, rage, anger, harsh words,
and slander, as well as all types of malicious behavior.
Ephesians 4:31 NLT

To blame others for our own problems is the height of futility. Yet blaming others is a favorite human pastime. Why? Because blaming is much easier than fixing, and criticizing others is so much easier than improving ourselves. So instead of solving our problems legitimately (by doing the work required to solve them), we are inclined to fret, to blame, and to criticize, while doing precious little else. When we do, our problems, quite predictably, remain unsolved.

As a woman with wisdom and experience, you know the blame game is seldom won. So it's your job to make sure your family understands that God has a way of helping those who help themselves, but He doesn't spend much time helping folks who spend more time blaming than working.

The willingness to accept responsibility
for one's own life is the source from which
self-respect springs.
Joan Didion

Never Stop Thanking Him

Bless the LORD, O my soul, and forget not all his benefits.
Psalm 103:2 KJV

As you begin another day, have you stopped to thank God for His blessings? And have you offered Him your heartfelt prayers and your whole-hearted praise? If so, you're a wise woman indeed. If not, it's time to slow down and offer a prayer of thanksgiving to the One who has given you life on earth and life eternal.

If you are a thoughtful grandmother, you will also be a thankful grandmother. After all, God has blessed you with a loving family, which in itself is a gift beyond compare. But it doesn't stop there. God has also blessed you in countless other ways.

You owe the Creator so much more than you can ever repay, and you owe Him your enduring gratitude. So thank Him . . . and keep thanking Him, today, tomorrow, and forever.

Sometimes, the hardest arithmetic to master is that which enables us to count our blessings.
Eric Hoffer

Still Learning?

How much better is it to get wisdom than gold!
and to get understanding rather to be chosen than silver!
Proverbs 16:16 KJV

Grandmother, here's a simple question: is your education complete? The correct answer is: of course not! Whether you're 45 or 105, you still have lots to learn, and that's good. The world is an exciting place for thoughtful people (like you) who continue to feed their brains a steady supply of good thoughts and new thoughts.

Education is the tool by which we come to know and appreciate the world in which we live. Education is not a luxury; it is a necessity and a powerful tool for good in this world. And it's a tool that we should use—and share—during every stage of life.

So if you think that your education is complete, think again. And if you think that class is dismissed, you're misinformed. To the contrary, school is never really out, because lifetime learning is both wonderful and essential. End of lecture.

True learning can take place at every age of life,
and it doesn't have to be in the curriculum plan.
Suzanne Dale Ezell

Forgiveness Now

Be merciful, just as your Father also is merciful.
Luke 6:36 HCSB

Forgiveness is seldom easy, but it is always right. When we forgive those who have hurt us, we honor God by obeying His commandments. But when we harbor bitterness against others, we disobey God—with predictably unhappy results.

Are you easily frustrated by the inevitable shortcomings of others? Are you a prisoner of bitterness or regret? Are you living in the past when you (and your loved ones) would be much better off if you lived in the present? If so, perhaps you need a refresher course in the art of forgiveness.

So here's a question for you, Grandmom: is there somebody out there you need to forgive? If so, today is the perfect day to do yourself a king-sized favor: forgive, forget, and move on. The sooner you rid your heart of bitterness, the sooner you can start filling it with more positive emotions—emotions like love.

Have you thought that your willingness
to forgive is really your affirmation
of the power of God to do you good?
Paula Rinehart

Distrust Negative Emotions

Now ye also put off all these; anger, wrath, malice . . .
Colossians 3:8 KJV

Sometimes, despite our best intentions, negative feelings can rob us of the peace and abundance that should be ours. When anger or anxiety separates us from the spiritual blessings that God has in store, we must rethink our priorities and renew our faith. And we must place faith above feelings. Human emotions are highly variable, decidedly unpredictable, and often unreliable. Our emotions are like the weather, only far more fickle. So we must learn to live by faith, not by the ups and downs of our own emotional roller coasters.

Sometime during this day, you will probably be gripped by a strong negative emotion. Distrust it. Reign it in. Test it. And turn it over to God. Your emotions will inevitably change; God will not. So trust Him completely as you watch your feelings slowly evaporate into thin air—which, of course, they will.

We need to be able to make decisions based on what we know rather than on what we feel.
Joyce Meyer

Embraced by the Father's Love

We love him, because he first loved us.
1 John 4:19 KJV

Every day of your life—indeed, every moment of your life—you are embraced by God. He is always with you, and His love for you and your family is deeper and more profound than you can imagine. And now, precisely because you are a wondrous creation treasured by God, a question presents itself: what will you do in response to God's love?

When you and your family members open yourselves to the Creator, you feel differently about yourselves, your neighbors, and your world. So here's your three-part challenge today, Grandmother: give thanks to the Father, accept His love, and encourage your family to do the same. When you do, you'll all be blessed.

Everything I possess of any worth
is a direct product of God's love.
Beth Moore

Take Time to Be Still

Be still, and know that I am God.
Psalm 46:10 KJV

A re you so busy that you rush through the day with scarcely a single moment for quiet contemplation and prayer? If so, it's time slow down and find time for quiet contemplation, or suffer the consequences.

You live in a society that seems to have the capacity to generate a near-infinite amount of noise. And every time somebody near you decides to crank up the volume, you may find yourself distracted, exasperated, infuriated, or all of the above. When you find your eardrums pounding and your heart doing the same, it's time to find a quiet place as quickly as possible and bask in the silence.

So today, Grandmother, find time to be still and claim the inner peace that accompanies silence . . . it's the peaceful way to live.

Be still, and in the quiet moments,
listen to the voice of your heavenly Father.
His words can renew your spirit—no one knows you and
your needs like He does.
Janet L. Weaver Smith

Seeking God

*You will seek me and find me when you seek me
with all your heart.*
Jeremiah 29:13 NIV

When we seek God with our hearts open and our prayers lifted, we need not look far: God is with us always.

Sometimes, however, in the crush of our daily duties, God may seem far away, but He is not. God is everywhere we have ever been and everywhere we will ever go. He is with us night and day; He knows our thoughts and our prayers. And when we earnestly seek Him, we will find Him, because He is here, waiting patiently for us to reach out to Him.

Today, Grandmother, reach out to the Giver of all blessings. Turn to Him for guidance and for strength. Remember that you, a woman who has been given so much, has every reason to welcome Him into your heart. And remember that no matter your circumstances, God never leaves you; He is here . . . always right here.

*Whenever you seek truth, you seek God,
whether or not you know it.*
Edith Stein

Your Gossip-Free Home

A person who gossips ruins friendships.
Proverbs 16:28 ICB

We human beings are sorely tempted to talk about one another. But gossip can have sad consequences and sometimes disastrous consequences. Furthermore, the Bible clearly instructs us that gossip is wrong. So the message that wise grandmothers teach is this: we must avoid the temptation to chatter about other folks behind their backs. After all, the cost of gossip always exceeds its worth.

As a concerned grandparent, it's up to you to make certain that your home is a gossip-free zone. When you do, you'll be teaching your family a valuable lesson, and you'll ensure that your home is a place where people are respected . . . and so are God's rules.

To belittle is to be little.
Author Unknown

God Is at Work

*The LORD will work out his plans for my life—
for your faithful love, O LORD, endures forever.*
Psalm 138:8 NLT

Whether you realize it or not, Grandmother, God is busily at work in your family. He has things He wants your family to do, and He has people He wants your family to help. Your assignment, should you choose to accept it, is to seek the will of God and follow it, wherever it may lead.

Sometimes God's plans are obvious to us, but at other times we may be genuinely puzzled about the direction our lives should take. In either case, we should consult our heavenly Father on a regular (spelled d-a-i-l-y) basis. And we should also consult trusted friends and family members who can help us discern God's will. When we do these things, God will make Himself known, and He will signify His approval by the blessings He bestows upon us and our loved ones.

*God has his reasons. He has His purposes.
Ours is an intentional God, brimming over with motive
and mission. He never does things capriciously or decides
with the flip of a coin.*
Joni Eareckson Tada

Negating Negativity

Don't pick on people, jump on their failures, criticize their faults—unless, of course, you want the same treatment. Don't condemn those who are down; that hardness can boomerang. Be easy on people; you'll find life a lot easier.
Luke 6:37 MSG

From experience, we know that it is easier to criticize than to correct. And we know that it is easier to find faults than solutions. Yet the urge to criticize others remains a powerful temptation for most of us. Our task—and what an important task it is—is to break the twin habits of negative thinking and critical speech.

Please remember, Grandmom, that negativity is highly contagious: we give it to others who, in turn, give it back to us. And remember that this cycle of negativity can be broken by positive thoughts, heartfelt prayers, and encouraging words.

As a thoughtful grandparent, you have a unique opportunity: the opportunity to extinguish unnecessary negativity within the four walls of your own home. So the next time you feel the urge to be critical or negative, think again. And keep thinking until you find something genuinely positive to contribute to your family and to your world.

Children have more need of models than critics.
Joseph Joubert

When It's Hard to Be Cheerful

Be cheerful. Keep things in good repair.
Keep your spirits up. Think in harmony. Be agreeable.
Do all that, and the God of love and peace
will be with you for sure.
2 Corinthians 13:11 MSG

On some days, as every woman knows, it's hard to be cheerful. Sometimes, as the demands of the world increase and your energy sags, you may feel less like cheering up and more like tearing up. But even during your toughest days, you can still discover pockets of cheerfulness if you look for them.

If you're taking yourself or your problems too seriously, it's time for an attitude adjustment. So lighten up and enjoy the occasional absurdities of everyday living. Learn to laugh with life. Keep searching for the thoughts, things, and people that can cheer you up. And make it a practice to count your blessings, not your misfortunes. When you seriously start searching for happiness, it really isn't that hard to find.

The path to cheerfulness is to sit cheerfully
and to act and speak as if cheerfulness
were already there.
William James

Do You Believe in Miracles?

With God's power working in us, God can do much, much more than anything we can ask or imagine.
Ephesians 3:20 NCV

Grandmother, do you believe in an all-powerful God who can do miraculous things in you and through you? You should. But perhaps, as you have faced the inevitable struggles of life here on earth, you have—without realizing it—placed limitations on God. To do so is a profound mistake. God's power has no such limitations, and He can work mighty miracles in your own life if you let Him.

Do you lack a firm faith in God's power to perform miracles for you and your loved ones? If so, you are attempting to place limitations on a God who has none. Instead of doubting your heavenly Father, you must place yourself in His hands. Instead of doubting God's power, you must trust it. Expect Him to work miracles, and be watchful. With God, absolutely nothing is impossible, including an amazing assortment of miracles that He stands ready, willing, and perfectly able to perform for you and yours.

God specializes in things thought impossible.
Catherine Marshall

Making the Grade Requires Work

*The one who plants and the one who waters
have the same purpose, and each will be
rewarded for his own work.*

1 Corinthians 3:8 NCV

Providing for a family requires work, and lots of it. And whether or not your work carries you outside the home, your good works have earned the gratitude of your loved ones and the praise of your heavenly Father.

Wise mothers and grandmothers know that it isn't easy to make the grade in today's competitive world. In fact, making the grade can be very difficult indeed. And the same can be said for the important work that occurs within the four walls of your home.

So whatever you choose to do, do it with commitment, with excitement, with enthusiasm, and with vigor. And then get ready for the rewards that are sure to come.

*I have found in work that you
only get back what you put into it,
but it does come back gift-wrapped.*

Joyce Brothers

What's Your Next Big Idea?

*May he give you the desire of your heart
and make all your plans succeed.*

Psalm 20:4 NIV

Okay, Grandmother, what's your next big idea? And before you answer that question, take a moment to consider the story of Ruth Handler. Ruth was a partner in a small business that made plastic items and a few toys. The little company was called Mattel. But everything changed in 1959 when Ruth observed her daughter Barbara pretending that paper dolls were grownups. That gave Ruth the idea for a grown-up doll she called Barbie in honor of her daughter. Since then, over a billion Barbie dolls have been sold—so many dolls, in fact, that Mattel has lost count.

Ruth Handler proved that good ideas are everywhere—we can even get them from our kids. So keep your eyes open for an idea that can change your world. When you do, you'll discover that new ideas (and fresh opportunities) are like Barbie dolls: they're simply too numerous to count.

*There is nothing as powerful as an idea
whose time has now come.*

Victor Hugo

Where Your Light Shines

You are the light of the world. A city on a hill cannot
be hidden. Neither do people light a lamp and put it under
a bowl. Instead they put it on its stand, and it gives
light to everyone in the house. In the same way,
let your light shine before men, that they may see your
good deeds and praise your Father in heaven.
Matthew 5:14–16 NIV

The Bible says, "You are the light of the world."
What kind of light have you been giving off?
Hopefully, you've been a good example for everybody,
starting with your family. Why? Because the world
needs all the light it can get, including yours!

Because you're a thoughtful grandmother, you
know that the example you set for your family and
friends is vitally important. In fact, everything you say
and do serves as a testimony to your life, your legacy,
and your faith.

So here's today's challenge, Grandmom: make
certain that your light—that particular light that you
and you alone can shine—is bright, clear, visible, and
pure. When you do, you'll most certainly light the
way for generations to come, which, by the way, is
precisely what your heavenly Father wants you to do.

If we do not radiate the light of Christ around us, the
sense of the darkness that prevails
in the world will increase.
Mother Teresa

Embracing Your Future

LORD, I turn my hope to You. My God, I trust in You.
Psalm 25:1–2 HCSB

Sometimes the future seems bright, and sometimes it does not. Yet even when we cannot see the possibilities of tomorrow, God can. Our challenge is to trust ourselves to do the best work we can, and then to trust God to do the rest.

When we trust God, we should trust Him without reservation. We should steel ourselves against the inevitable disappointments of the day, secure in the knowledge that our heavenly Father has a plan for the future that is brighter than we can imagine.

Are you willing to look to the future with trust and confidence? Hopefully so, because the future should not be feared; it should be embraced. And it most certainly should be embraced by you.

Live for today, but hold your hands open to tomorrow. Anticipate the future and its changes with joy. There is a seed of God's love in every event, every circumstance, every unpleasant situation in which you may find yourself.

Barbara Johnson

Giving Lots of Encouragement to Family and Friends

Shepherd the flock of God which is among you.
1 Peter 5:2 NKJV

Life is a team sport, and all of us need occasional pats on the back from our teammates. Whether you realize it or not, many of the people you encounter each day are in desperate need of a smile or an encouraging word. The world can be a difficult place, and countless friends and family members may be troubled by the challenges of everyday life.

Since you don't always know who needs your help, the best strategy is to try to encourage all the people who cross your path. So today, Grandmother, make this promise to yourself and keep it: vow to be a world-class source of encouragement to everyone you meet. Share your optimism with family members, friends, coworkers, and even with strangers. Never has the need been greater.

Giving encouragement to others is a most welcome gift, for the results of it are lifted spirits, increased self-worth, and a hopeful future.
Florence Littauer

Too Busy?

Don't burn out; keep yourselves fueled and aflame.
Be alert servants of the Master, cheerfully expectant.
Don't quit in hard times; pray all the harder.
Romans 12:11–12 MSG

It's been said before, but it's worth saying again: things that matter most must never be at the mercy of things which matter least. And now, with that said, how will you choose to organize the busy day ahead? Will you rush from place to place with scarcely a moment to spare, or will you slow yourself down to make time for the things that really matter?

The world might have you believe that there's enough time to "have it all"—that there's plenty of time to meet every obligation and finish every task. But there isn't enough time for everything, so it's up to you, Grandmother, to invest your life in the important things.

Today, before you rush headlong into the fray, take a few moments to think about your real priorities . . . and plan your day accordingly.

Does God care about all the responsibilities
we have to juggle in our daily lives? Of course.
But he cares more that our lives demonstrate balance, the
ability to discern what is essential
and give ourselves fully to it.
Penelope Stokes

December

Thank-You Hug for Grandmother

Dear Grandmother,

   As the Christmas season rolls around yet again, we thank you for holidays past—for all the things you did to fill those memory-making moments with laughter and excitement. Holidays sometimes have a way of getting out of control, but even on those days when you were overworked and overstressed, you kept the holiday spirit, and we noticed. And we will never forget.

God's Timing

Wait for the LORD; be courageous
and let your heart be strong. Wait for the LORD.
Psalm 27:14 HCSB

If you're in a hurry for good things to happen to you and your family, you're not the only grandmother on the block who feels that way. But sometimes you'll simply have to be patient.

God has created a world that unfolds according to His own timetable, not ours . . . thank goodness! We mortals might make a terrible mess of things. God does not.

Of course, God's plans do not always unfold according to our own wishes, or at the time of our own choosing. Nonetheless, we should trust the benevolent, all-knowing Father as we wait patiently for Him to reveal Himself. Until God's plans are made clear to us, we must walk in faith and never lose hope, knowing that His plans are always best. Always.

The deepest spiritual lessons are not learned by His letting us have our way in the end, but by His making us wait, bearing with us in love and patience until we are able honestly to pray what He taught His disciples to pray: Thy will be done.
Elisabeth Elliot

Very Big Dreams for You and Your Family

It is pleasant to see dreams come true.
Proverbs 13:19 NLT

It takes courage to dream big dreams—dreams for yourself and your family. You'll discover the courage to dream big when you do three things: accept the past, trust God to handle the future, and make the most of the time He has given you today.

Are you excited about the opportunities of today and thrilled by the possibilities of tomorrow? Do you confidently expect God to lead you and yours to a place of abundance, peace, and joy? If you trust God's promises, you should believe that your future is intensely and eternally bright.

Today, promise yourself that you'll do your family (and the world) a king-sized favor by wholeheartedly pursuing your dreams. After all, no dreams are too big for God—not even a grandmother's. So start living—and dreaming—accordingly.

You cannot out-dream God.
John Eldredge

First, You Make Your Habits

*John said, "Change your hearts and lives because
the kingdom of heaven is near."*
Matthew 3:2 NCV

You've heard it said on many occasions: first, you make your habits, and then your habits make you. Some habits will inevitably bring you closer to God; other habits will lead you away from the path He has chosen for you. If you sincerely desire to improve your spiritual health, you must honestly examine the habits that make up the fabric of your day. And you must abandon those habits that are harming you. So here's a word to the wise: if you want to improve your life, improve your habits.

Grandmother, you have the power to create a new, healthier, happier you. Exercise that power by taking control of your life today. When you do, you'll put your new habits to work for you . . . and you'll be a powerful example to your family, to your friends, and to the world.

*If you want to form a new habit, get to work.
If you want to break a bad habit,
get on your knees.*
Marie T. Freeman

Love Is a Choice

May mercy, peace, and love be multiplied to you.
Jude 1:2 HCSB

Love is a choice. Either you choose to behave lovingly toward others . . . or not; either you behave yourself in ways that enhance your relationships . . . or not. But make no mistake: genuine love requires effort. Simply put, if you wish to build lasting relationships, you must be willing to do your part.

God does not intend for you to experience mediocre relationships; He created you for far greater things. Building lasting relationships requires compassion, wisdom, empathy, kindness, courtesy, and forgiveness. If that sounds like work, it is—which is perfectly fine with God. Why? Because He knows that you are capable of doing that work, and because He knows that the fruits of your labors will enrich the lives of your loved ones and the lives of generations yet unborn.

*Life is immortal, love eternal; death is nothing
but a horizon, and a horizon is only
the limit of our vision.*
Corrie ten Boom

When Your Courage Is Tested

*Be strong and courageous,
all you who put your hope in the LORD.*
Psalm 31:24 HCSB

Even the most optimistic grandmother on the planet may find her courage tested by the inevitable disappointments and tragedies of life. After all, we live in a world filled with uncertainty, hardship, sickness, and danger. Old Man Trouble, it seems, is never too far from the front door.

When we focus upon our fears and our doubts, we may find many reasons to lie awake at night and fret about the uncertainties of the coming day. A better strategy, of course, is to focus not upon our fears, but instead upon our God.

So, Grandmother, here's a hint: don't direct your thoughts to worst-case scenarios, and don't focus too intently on your fears. Instead, trust God's plan and His eternal love for you. And remember: whatever the size of your challenge, God is bigger.

*I have found the perfect antidote for fear.
Whenever it sticks up its ugly face,
I clobber it with prayer.*
Dale Evans Rogers

High Expectations

Your beliefs about these things should be kept secret between you and God. People are happy if they can do what they think is right without feeling guilty.

Romans 14:22 NCV

Expectations, expectations, expectations! As a dues-paying citizen of the twenty-first century, you know that demands can be high and expectations even higher. The media delivers an endless stream of messages that tells you how to look, how to behave, how to eat, and how to dress. The media's expectations are impossible to meet—God's are not. God doesn't expect perfection . . . and neither should you.

The difference between perfectionism and realistic expectations is the difference between a life of frustration and a life of contentment. So if you or your family members are bound up by the chains of perfectionism, it's time to ask yourselves who you're trying to impress, and why.

Your first responsibility is to the heavenly Father who created you. Then you bear a powerful responsibility to your family. But when it comes to meeting society's unrealistic expectations, forget it!

Do not lose courage in considering your own imperfections.

St. Francis of Sales

Emotional Quicksand

*All bitterness, anger and wrath, insult and slander
must be removed from you, along with all wickedness.
And be kind and compassionate
to one another, forgiving one another.*

Ephesians 4:31–32 HCSB

Are you mired in the quicksand of bitterness or regret? If so, it's time to free yourself from the mire. The world holds few if any rewards for those who remain angrily focused upon the past. Still, the act of forgiveness is difficult for all but the most saintly men and women.

Being frail, fallible, imperfect human beings, most of us are quick to anger, quick to blame, slow to forgive, and even slower to forget. Yet we know that it's best to forgive others, just as we, too, have been forgiven.

If there exists even one person—including yourself—against whom you still harbor bitter feelings, it's time to forgive and move on. Bitterness and regret are not parts of God's plan for you, but He won't force you to forgive others. It's a job that only you can finish, and the sooner you finish it, the better.

*Forgiveness is the key that unlocks the door of resentment
and the handcuffs of hate.
It is a power that breaks the chains of bitterness
and the shackles of selfishness.*

Corrie ten Boom

Too Much Media?

> *We must obey God rather than men.*
> Acts 5:29 HCSB

The media is working around the clock in an attempt to rearrange your family's priorities in ways that may not always be in your best interests. All too often, the media teaches your family that physical appearance is all-important, that material possessions should be acquired at any cost, and that the world operates independently of God's laws. But guess what? Those messages are untrue.

So here's an important question, Grandmother: will you control what appears on your TV screen, or will your family be controlled by it? If you're willing to take complete control over the images that appear inside the four walls of your home, you'll be doing your clan a king-sized favor.

So today, with no further delay, take control of your family's clicker. You'll be glad you did, and so, in a few years, will they.

> *The popular media has a way of attacking*
> *your senses and your heart.*
> *Approach the media with care.*
> Marie T. Freeman

Teaching Them to Manage Time

*If you are too lazy to plow in the right season,
you will have no food at the harvest.*

Proverbs 20:4 NLT

Grandmother, are you serious about teaching your grandchildren the wisdom of getting things done sooner rather than later? And are you willing to teach the gospel of "getting things done" by your example as well as your words? If so, your grandkids will be the better for it.

Procrastination is, at its core, a struggle against oneself; the only antidote is action. Once we acquire the habit of doing what needs to be done when it needs to be done, we avoid untold trouble, worry, and stress. We learn to defeat procrastination by paying less attention to our fears and more attention to our responsibilities.

Life punishes procrastinators, and it does so sooner rather than later. In other words, Grandmom, life doesn't procrastinate. And neither should we.

*Lost time is like a run in a stocking.
It always gets worse.*

Anne Morrow Lindbergh

Integrity Now

The godly walk with integrity;
blessed are their children after them.
Proverbs 20:7 NLT

One of the great gifts a grandmother can give to her family is the opportunity of witnessing a grown-up woman face life's inevitable ups and downs with unwavering integrity.

Wise women understand that integrity is a crucial building block in the foundation of a well-lived life. Integrity is a precious thing—difficult to build, but easy to tear down; savvy women (of all ages) value it and protect it at all costs.

Living a life of integrity isn't always the easiest way, but it is always the right way. And God clearly intends that it should be your way too. So today, as you preach the gospel of integrity to your family, preach it with your words and your actions, with a decided emphasis on the latter.

If you want to be proactive in the way you live your life, if you want to influence your life's direction, if you want your life to exhibit the qualities you find desirable, and if you want to live with integrity, then you need to know what your values are, decide to embrace them, and practice them every day.

John Maxwell

God's To-Do List

Be energetic in your life of salvation, reverent and sensitive
before God. That energy is God's energy, an energy
deep within you, God himself willing and working
at what will give him the most pleasure.
Philippians 2:12–13 MSG

If you're a grandmother with too many demands and too few hours in which to meet them, you are in good company. Whether you're a young grandma or a seasoned senior, you know that caring for a family is, without a doubt, one of the world's most demanding professions. So it's easy to become overwhelmed from time to time.

What's a woman to do? Well, you can start by making sure that you don't overcommit yourself (which means you'll probably need to start saying no a little more often). Next, you should tackle your responsibilities in the approximate order of their importance (first things first). Finally, after you've done your best, you should turn everything else over to your Creator.

You can be sure that God will give you the energy to do the most important things on today's to-do list if you ask Him. So ask Him . . . starting right now.

The task ahead of us is never as great as
the Power behind us.
Author Unknown

He Is Love

> *God is love, and the one who remains in love*
> *remains in God, and God remains in him.*
> 1 John 4:16 HCSB

God is love—it's a broad and sweeping statement, and it's a profoundly important description of who God is and how God works. God's love is perfect. When we open our hearts to Him, we are touched by the Creator's hand, and we are transformed.

Sometimes we don't spend much time thinking about God or His love. Instead, we focus on the obligations and distractions of everyday living. But when we pause to compare the size of our problems to the size of God's love, we are comforted.

So today, even if you can only carve out a few quiet moments, offer sincere prayers of thanksgiving to your Father. Thank Him for His blessings, for His gifts, and for His love. But not necessarily in that order.

> *Knowing God's sovereignty and unconditional love*
> *imparts a beauty to life . . . and to you.*
> Kay Arthur

No Burden Too Heavy

*These things I have spoken to you, that in Me you may
have peace. In the world you will have tribulation;
but be of good cheer, I have overcome the world.*
John 16:33 NKJV

As we travel the roads of life, all of us are confronted
with streets that seem to be dead ends. When
we are, we may become discouraged. After all, we
live in a society where expectations can be high and
demands even higher.

If you find yourself enduring difficult circumstances or profound disappointments, remember that
God remains in His heaven, remember that He is
watching over you, and remember that He will never
ask you to carry a load that's too heavy for you.

So, Grandmother, the next time you're asked to
shoulder a heavy maternal burden, remember that
there is a good way and a bad way to carry every load.
The best way is to keep working, keep believing, and
never give in to discouragement. And remember this:
no load is too heavy if you discover the right way to
carry it, but no load's too light if you don't.

*The size of your burden is never as important
as the way you carry it.*
Lena Horne

December 14

If You Become Discouraged

Do not be afraid or discouraged, for the LORD
will personally go ahead of you. He will be with you;
he will neither fail you nor abandon you.

Deuteronomy 31:8 NLT

Even the most upbeat grandparents can become discouraged, and you are no exception. After all, you live in a world where expectations are usually high, higher, or highest. And if, for any reason, you fall short, you can start feeling blue in a hurry . . . but blue feelings are unlikely to solve anything.

The next time you face a big-time disappointment, face it head on. Don't give in, and don't give up. Instead, assess your situation realistically and try to improve upon it. And while you're at it, have a sincere chat with God, because He probably has a thing or two to tell you.

God asks you to distrust your fears and, instead, to trust Him. He is a God of possibility, not negativity. You can be sure that He will guide you through your difficulties and beyond them . . . far beyond.

If I am asked how we are to get rid of discouragements, I
can only say, as I have had to say of so many other wrong
spiritual habits, we must give them up. It is never worth
while to argue against discouragement. There is only one
argument that can meet it, and that is the argument of
God.

Hannah Whitall Smith

You Are the Light of Your Family

You are the light that gives light to the world.
In the same way, you should be a light for other people.
Live so that they will see the good things you do
and will praise your Father in heaven.
Matthew 5:14,16 NCV

Our children learn from us in two ways: from the lessons we teach and from the lives we live. But not necessarily in that order. When it comes to teaching, demonstration trumps proclamation.

What kind of example are you? Are you the kind of grandmother whose life serves as a genuine example of patience and righteousness? Are you a woman whose behavior serves as a positive role model for others? Are you the kind of grandmom whose actions, day in and day out, are based upon kindness, faithfulness, and a sincere love for the Lord? If so, you are not only blessed by God, but you are also a powerful force for good in a world—and in a family—that desperately needs positive influences such as yours.

The mother is and must be, whether she knows it
or not, the greatest, strongest,
and most lasting teacher her children have.
Hannah Whitall Smith

A Passion for Life

He did it with all his heart. So he prospered.
2 Chronicles 31:21 NKJV

When people become passionate about life, great things start to happen. So here's the big question for you, Grandmother: are you passionate about your faith, your family, and your future? If so, you can expect the world to share your enthusiasm. But if you make the mistake of allowing pessimism and doubt to become permanent guests at your house, it's time for a heart-to-heart talk with your Father in heaven.

God has big plans for you and your family, plans for a glorious future that only He can see. So if you ever feel the passion slowly draining from your life, it's time to refocus your thoughts, your energies, and your prayers . . . starting, of course, with your prayers. And then get ready for great things to happen.

Get absolutely enthralled with something.
Throw yourself into it with abandon.
Get out of yourself. Be somebody. Do something.
Norman Vincent Peale

Optimism Now

Make me to hear joy and gladness.

Psalm 51:8 KJV

Are you an optimistic, hopeful, enthusiastic grandparent? I hope so. But sometimes you may find yourself pulled down by the inevitable demands and worries of life here on earth. If you find yourself discouraged, exhausted, or both, then it's time to take your concerns to God. When you do, He will lift your spirits and renew your strength.

This day offers yet another opportunity to celebrate the life God has given you. Seize that opportunity. Count your blessings and give thanks for them. Do your best to turn stumbling blocks into stepping stones. Make up your mind to think optimistically about your life, your family, and your future.

When you stop to think about it, this world is, indeed, a miraculous place. And God remains in His heaven. And you are blessed, now and forever. So with these thoughts in mind, be optimistic. Now.

A pessimist is one who makes difficulties of his opportunities; an optimist is one who makes opportunities of his difficulties.

Harry S Truman

Making Better Decisions

*If any of you lacks wisdom, he should ask God,
who gives to all generously and without criticizing,
and it will be given to him.*

James 1:5 HCSB

Decisions, decisions, decisions. So many decisions to make, and with so little information. Yet decide we must. The stories of our lives are, quite literally, human dramas woven together by the habits we form and the choices we make.

The quality of the decisions you make today will determine, to a surprising extent, the quality of this particular day and the direction of all the ones that follow it.

Are you willing to invest the time, the effort, and the prayers that are required to make wise decisions? Are you willing to take your concerns to God and to avail yourself of the messages and mentors He has placed along your path? If you answered yes to these questions, you'll most certainly make better decisions, decisions that, by the way, will lead directly and inexorably to a better life.

*The location of your affections will drive
the direction of your decisions.*

Lisa Bevere

December 19

Never Stop Growing

*When I was a child, I spoke and thought
and reasoned as a child does. But when I grew up,
I put away childish things.*
1 Corinthians 13:11 NLT

If we wish to grow intellectually and spiritually, we need both knowledge and wisdom. Knowledge is found in textbooks. Wisdom, on the other hand, is found through experience, through years of trial and error, and through careful attention to the Word of God. Knowledge is an important building block in a well-lived life, and it pays rich dividends both personally and professionally. But, wisdom is even more important because it refashions not only our minds but also our hearts.

When it comes to your faith, God doesn't intend for you to stand still. He wants you to keep growing as a woman, as a grandmother, and as a spiritual being. No matter how grown-up you may be, you still have growing to do. And the more you grow, the more beautiful you become, inside and out.

*God will help us become the people
we are meant to be, if only we will ask Him.*
Hannah Whitall Smith

Celebrating His Gifts

*Set your minds on what is above,
not on what is on the earth.*

Colossians 3:2 HCSB

Life is a gift from God, a gift with eternal possibilities. Every day should be celebrated as a priceless gift from the Creator. So here's a question for you, Grandmother: will you celebrate today? Hopefully, you'll answer with a resounding "Yes"!

This day is a nonrenewable resource—once it's gone, it's gone forever. So celebrate the life that God has given you by thinking optimistically about yourself, your family, your day, and your future. Give thanks to the One who has showered you and yours with blessings, and trust in your heart that He wants to give you so much more.

*Attitude is the mind's paintbrush;
it can color any situation.*

Barbara Johnson

Never Put Your Dreams on Hold

Delayed hope makes the heart sick.
Proverbs 13:12 HCSB

She was born in rural Mississippi and lived with her grandmother in a house that had no indoor plumbing. She made it to college in Nashville, where she got her start in television. Over time, she moved to the top of her profession, and today her show, *The Oprah Winfrey Show,* is an unparalleled hit.

When questioned about her journey to the top, Oprah says, "God can dream a bigger dream than we can dream for ourselves." And she is right. So try Oprah's formula for success: increase the size of your dreams. The good Lord's plan for each of us is big, very big, but it's up to us to accept the part, to step up on stage, and to perform.

Too many people put their dreams "on hold."
It takes an uncommon amount of guts to put your dreams
on the line, to hold them up and say,
"How good or bad am I?"
That's where the courage comes in.
Erma Bombeck

Life on Its Own Terms

> *People may make plans in their minds,*
> *but the Lord decides what they will do.*
>
> Proverbs 16:9 NCV

Sometimes we must accept life on its terms, not our own. Life has a way of unfolding, not as we will, but as it will. And sometimes there is precious little we can do to change things.

When events transpire that are beyond our control, we have a choice: we can either learn the art of acceptance, or we can make ourselves miserable as we struggle to change the unchangeable.

We must entrust the things we cannot change to God. Once we have done so, we can prayerfully and faithfully tackle the important work that He has placed before us: doing something about the things we can change . . . and doing it sooner rather than later.

Can you summon the courage and the wisdom to accept life on its own terms? If so, Grandmother, you and your family will most certainly be rewarded for your good judgment.

> *Life is not always what one wants it to be,*
> *but to make the best of it, as it is,*
> *is the only way of being happy.*
>
> Jenny Jerome Churchill

Honoring the Family

*If a kingdom is divided against itself,
that kingdom cannot stand. If a house is divided
against itself, that house cannot stand.*

Mark 3:24–25 HCSB

Grandmother, as you consider God's purpose for your own life, you must also consider how your plans will affect the most important people God has entrusted to your care: your family.

Even when they are separated by distance and time, our loved ones never really leave us. They are always with us in our hearts and in our prayers.

Our families are precious gifts from the Creator; we must care for our loved ones and make time for them, even when the demands of the day are great. In a world filled with countless obligations and frequent frustrations, we may be tempted to take our families and friends for granted. But God intends otherwise. God intends that we honor Him by honoring our loved ones—by giving them our support, our time, and our cooperation.

*Our Creator, who divided the year into seasons and the
days into mornings and nights, also divided people into
families. He created this gift of
a structure to offer stability and loving security
in the midst of an unstable and insecure world.*

Carol Kuykendall

No Time Like the Present

> *Companions as we are in this work with you,*
> *we beg you, please don't squander one bit of this*
> *marvelous life God has given us.*
>
> 2 Corinthians 6:1 MSG

You've heard it said on hundreds of occasions: There's no time like the present. It's a cliché that lots of people seem to agree with, and why shouldn't they? After all, it's also a cliché that's true.

If you want something done, Grandmother, do it now. If not, tell yourself that you're going to get around to it some day (knowing full well that if you're like most folks, that "some day" may never actually arrive).

You have plenty of responsibilities, but not all responsibilities are created equal. So it's up to you to fulfill your most important duties (like taking care of your family) first and finish up the less important jobs later—if and when you ever get around to them. Father's orders.

> *Whatever I'm doing, I don't think in terms of tomorrow. I*
> *try to live in the present moment.*
>
> Anita Baker

Cultivating God's Gifts

I remind you to fan into flame the gift of God.
2 Timothy 1:6 NIV

All women possess special gifts, talents, and opportunities; you are no exception. But your skills and opportunities are no guarantee of success; they must be cultivated and nurtured; otherwise, they will go unused . . . and God's gifts to you will be lost.

Today, be a grandmother who accepts this challenge: value the talent that God has given you, nourish it, make it grow, and share it with the world. And while you're at it, do your best to help your loved ones do the same. After all, if you really want to thank God for the talents and opportunities He has entrusted to you, the very best way to express your gratitude to the Giver is to use wisely—even reverently—the gifts He has given you.

All of us attain the greatest success and happiness possible in this life whenever we use our native capacities to their fullest extent.
Smiley Blanton

Making Peace with the Past

Do not remember the past events, pay no attention to things of old. Look, I am about to do something new; even now it is coming. Do you not see it? Indeed, I will make a way in the wilderness, rivers in the desert.

Isaiah 43:18–19 HCSB

Have you made peace with your past? If so, congratulations. But if you are mired in the quicksand of regret, it's time to plan your escape. How can you do so? By accepting what has been and by trusting God for what will be.

Because you are human, you may be slow to forget yesterday's disappointments; if so, you are not alone. But if you sincerely seek to focus your hopes and energies on the future, then you must find ways to accept the past, no matter how difficult it may be to do so.

So, Grandmother, if you have not yet made peace with the past, today is the day to declare an end to all hostilities. When you do, you can then turn your thoughts to wondrous promises of God and to the glorious future that He has in store for you.

There is no road back to yesterday.

Oswald Chambers

Beyond Anger

When you are angry, do not sin, and be sure to stop
being angry before the end of the day.
Do not give the devil a way to defeat you.
Ephesians 4:26–27 NCV

Perhaps God gave each of us one mouth and two ears in order that we might listen twice as much as we speak. Unfortunately, many of us do otherwise, especially when we become angry.

Sometime today you may be tempted to respond in anger to a family member, to a friend, to a coworker, or even to a complete stranger. Don't do it! Instead of doing the impulsive thing, do the hard (and wise) thing: control your temper before your temper controls you.

As the old saying goes, "Anger usually improves nothing but the arch of a cat's back." So don't allow resentment to rule your life, Grandmother, or, for that matter, your day. Chronic anger is spiritual poison. Please don't ever let it poison you.

When something robs you of your peace of mind, ask
yourself if it is worth the energy you are expending on it. If
not, then put it out of your mind in an act of discipline.
Every time the thought
of "it" returns, refuse it.
Kay Arthur

Who Can You Hug Today?

A merry heart doeth good like a medicine:
but a broken spirit drieth the bones.
Proverbs 17:22 KJV

Who can you hug today? If your kids and grandkids are nearby, this may be the easiest question you've ever had to answer, because your youngsters always need a hug (or two). But the hugging needn't stop with kids, grandkids, husbands, and close relatives.

Today, you'll probably bump into quite a few folks who would appreciate an outstretched hand or a pat on the back or a full-body bear hug. And if you don't slow down to offer a kind word or a heartfelt hug, who will?

So here's your challenge for today: find at least five people who need a hug (or two) from you. And then do the right thing: hug with abandon. When you do, you'll discover that although a hug costs nothing, it's priceless.

A hug is the ideal gift . . . one size fits all.
Author Unknown

Measuring Your Words

Do you see people who speak too quickly?
There is more hope for a foolish person than for them.
Proverbs 29:20 NCV

God's Word reminds us that "Reckless words pierce like a sword, but the tongue of the wise brings healing" (Proverbs 12:18 NIV). So, Grandmother, if you seek to be a source of encouragement to friends or family members, then you must measure your words carefully. And that's exactly what God wants you to do.

Today, make this promise to yourself: vow to be an honest, effective, encouraging communicator at work, at home, and everyplace in between. Speak wisely, not impulsively. Use words of kindness and praise, not words of anger or derision. Learn how to be truthful without being cruel. Remember that you have the power to heal others or to injure them, to lift others up or to hold them back. And when you learn how to lift them up, you'll soon discover that you've lifted yourself up too.

Keeping the lines of communication open can help exterminate the pests that gnaw away at love.
Annie Chapman

The Gift of Eternal Life

God so loved the world that He gave
His only begotten Son, that whoever believes in Him
should not perish but have everlasting life.
John 3:16 NKJV

Your ability to envision the future, like your life here on earth, is limited. God's vision, however, is not burdened by any such limitations. He sees all things, He knows all things, and His plans for you endure for all time.

God's plans are not limited to the events of life here on earth. Your heavenly Father has bigger things in mind for you . . . much bigger things. So praise the Creator for the gift of eternal life, and share the good news with all who cross your path. And please don't forget, Grandmother, that your Creator has invited you to join Him for all eternity. You belong to the Father—today, tomorrow, and forever.

God loves you and wants you to experience peace and
life—abundant and eternal.
Billy Graham

A Final Thank You

Her children stand and bless her.
Proverbs 31:28 NLT

Dear Grandmother,

Thank you for the love, the care, the work, the discipline, the wisdom, the support, and the faith. Thanks for being a concerned grandparent and a worthy example. Thanks for giving life and for teaching it. Thanks for being patient with us, even when you were tired, or frustrated—or both. Thanks for babysitting, baking cookies, telling stories, and wiping away tears. And thanks for being a wonderful, wise woman, a woman worthy of our admiration and our love.

Thank you, Grandmother, for the precious hugs you gave us then, and for the precious memories we still treasure today. You have earned a great big hug from us, too, but you've earned so much more. You deserve our family's undying gratitude and love. May you enjoy God's blessings always, and may you never, ever forget how much we love you.

Signed,
Your Loving Family

Notes

These pages have been provided
for your personal journaling and meditation.

Notes

Notes

Notes

Notes

Notes

Notes

Notes

Scripture References

Scripture quotations marked HCSB have been taken from the Holman Christian Standard Bible®, copyright © 1999, 2000, 2002, 2003 by Holman Bible Publishers. Used by permission.

Scripture quotations marked ICB are taken from the International Children's Bible®, copyright © 1986, 1988, 1999 by Tommy Nelson™, a division of Thomas Nelson, Inc., Nashville, Tennessee 37214. Used by permission.

Scripture quotations marked KJV are taken from the Holy Bible, King James Version.

Scripture quotations marked TLB are taken from The Living Bible, copyrighted ©1971. Used by permission of Tyndale House Publishers, Inc. Wheaton, Illinois 60189. All rights reserved.

Scripture quotations marked MSG are taken from The Message. Copyright © 1993, 1994, 1995, 1996, 2000, 2001, 2002. Used by permission of NavPress Publishing Group.

Scripture quotations marked NASB are taken from the New American Standard Bible, © 1960, 1962, 1963, 1968, 1971, 1972, 1973, 1975, 1977, by The Lockman Foundation. Used by permission.

Scripture quotations marked NCV are taken from the New Century Version®. Copyright © 1987, 1988, 1991 by Thomas Nelson, Inc. Used by permission. All rights reserved.

Scripture quotations marked NIV are taken from the Holy Bible, New International Version®. Copyright © 1973, 1978, 1984 by International Bible Society. Used by permission of Zondervan Publishing House. All rights reserved.

Scripture quotations marked NKJV are taken from the Holy Bible, New King James Version. Copyright © 1982, 1988 by Thomas Nelson, Inc. All rights reserved.

Scripture quotations marked NLT are taken from the Holy Bible, New Living Translation, copyright © 1996. Used by permission of Tyndale House Publishers, Inc., Wheaton, Illinois 60189. All rights reserved.

Need more **Hugs** in your life?

Three hundred sixty-five daily inspirations offer soothing words of peace, courage, and comfort to uplift the spirit.

Three hundred sixty-five daily devotions encourage and uplift moms every day of the year.

A perfect way to start the day with 365 daily devotions to inspire women.

This book contains collected messages of assurance, blessing, and hope designed to encourage the soul with the promises found in God's Word.

For a complete list of Hugs books visit
Christian.SimonandSchuster.com